HETZER vs SU-76M

Hungary 1945

PETER SAMSONOV

OSPREY PUBLISHING
Bloomsbury Publishing Plc
Kemp House, Chawley Park, Cumnor Hill, Oxford OX2 9PH, UK
Bloomsbury Publishing Ireland Limited,
29 Earlsfort Terrace, Dublin 2, D02 AY28, Ireland
1385 Broadway, 5th Floor, New York, NY 10018, USA
E-mail: info@ospreypublishing.com
www.ospreypublishing.com

OSPREY is a trademark of Osprey Publishing Ltd

First published in Great Britain in 2025

© Osprey Publishing Ltd, 2025

All rights reserved. No part of this publication may be: i) reproduced or transmitted in any form, electronic or mechanical, including photocopying, recording or by means of any information storage or retrieval system without prior permission in writing from the publishers; or ii) used or reproduced in any way for the training, development or operation of artificial intelligence (AI) technologies, including generative AI technologies. The rights holders expressly reserve this publication from the text and data mining exception as per Article 4(3) of the Digital Single Market Directive (EU) 2019/790

A catalogue record for this book is available from the British Library.

ISBN: PB 9781472866103; eBook 9781472866110;
ePDF 9781472866080; XML 9781472866097

25 26 27 28 29   10 9 8 7 6 5 4 3 2 1

Maps by bounford.com
Index by Rob Munro
Typeset by Lumina Datamatics Ltd.
Printed by Repro India Ltd.

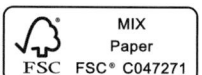

Osprey Publishing supports the Woodland Trust, the UK's leading woodland conservation charity.

To find out more about our authors and books visit www.ospreypublishing.com. Here you will find extracts, author interviews, details of forthcoming events and the option to sign up for our newsletter.

For product safety related questions contact productsafety@bloomsbury.com

Author's note

A note on the terminology used in this book: the vehicles in question were referred to by different names, including nicknames. While the name 'Hetzer' (persistence hunter: a type of hunter that pursues a prey to exhaustion rather than engaging it in direct confrontation) was not used in official documents, its use by front-line troops is a recorded fact and today the vehicle is most commonly referred to by this name rather than its official designation.
For this reason, discussions of front-line service in this book use the term 'Jagdpanzer 38' and 'Hetzer' interchangeably, while technical discussions refer to specific variants (Jagdpanzer 38, G-13, ST-I, etc.). Likewise, while the designation changed from SU-76 to SU-76M in technical documentation, this change was of little importance to front-line Red Army troops. The tactical role of the SPG remained the same, and, as a rule, front-line documents continued to refer to the vehicle as the SU-76 with no distinction between the old and new models. This book keeps to this style, using the terms 'SU-76' and 'SU-76M' where appropriate in technical descriptions and simply 'SU-76' in discussions of tactics and combat.

Editor's note

All measurements of the angle of armour in this book are expressed in degrees from vertical.

Title-page photograph: Soviet armour, including SU-76Ms, destroyed at Székesfehérvár. Fighting in January and February 1945 bloodied the 3rd Ukrainian Front and made it a prime candidate for a follow-up Axis attack. (Süddeutsche Zeitung/Alamy Stock Photo)

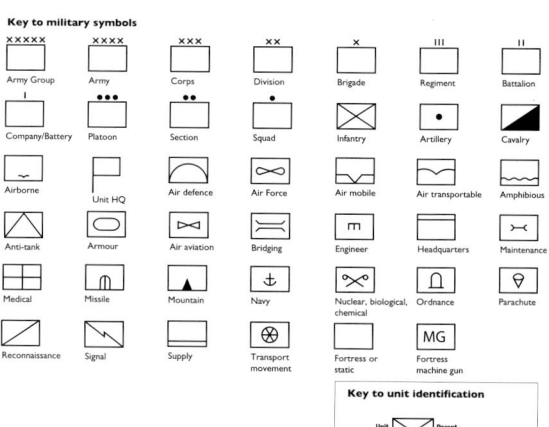

CONTENTS

Introduction	4
Chronology	7
Design and Development	8
The Strategic Situation	24
Technical Specifications	30
The Combatants	46
Combat	55
Statistics and Analysis	71
Aftermath	75
Glossary	78
Bibliography	78
Index	80

INTRODUCTION

Armour was always the ace up the sleeve of the Nazi-era German armed forces. Armoured spearheads were instrumental to the rapid defeat of Poland in 1939 and France in 1940. Armour was the backbone of the bold long-range thrusts that made a name for Generalleutnant Erwin Rommel in North Africa. The way to Moscow in 1941 was paved by four massive Panzer groups. Even after the Red Army stopped them just short of the Soviet capital, the Panzerwaffe was reborn by the following summer, carrying out a campaign of equally impressive scope and speed towards the south, where Stalingrad and the oilfields of the Caucasus lay as a tempting prize. The Panzers were stopped once more, again at an enormous cost paid in blood and steel.

The Germans could not repeat the same trick for a third time, however. Operation *Zitadelle* (the battle of Kursk) failed to yield the same results as Operation *Barbarossa* (the invasion of the Soviet Union in the summer of 1941) and *Fall Blau* (Case Blue, the battle of Stalingrad in the summer of 1942). Seemingly stronger than ever and equipped with new and powerful heavy tanks and tank destroyers, the German armed forces only made a dent in the defences of the Kursk Salient.

Rather than cutting off and eliminating a huge swathe of Soviet troops as the Germans had done so many times in 1941, Hitler's forces found themselves first defending and then retreating, chased all the way to the Dnieper River. No German offensive materialized in the summer of 1944 either, as Heeresgruppe Mitte (Army Group Centre) disintegrated in a matter of weeks under the steamroller of Operation *Bagration*.

By 1945 the Panzerwaffe was a shadow of its former self, but far from beaten. As the number of Germany's allies dwindled, it was decided to make a stand in Hungary near Lake Balaton. If successful, Operation *Frühlingserwachen* (*Spring Awakening*) would see the 3rd Ukrainian Front of the Red Army, 1st Bulgarian Army and

An SU-76M during urban combat, early 1945. (Victor Temin/Slava Katamidze Collection/Getty Images)

3rd Yugoslavian Army pushed back to the Danube River, preventing any further advance into Hungary, Austria and Germany's southern regions. The Panzerwaffe would once again be the backbone of this offensive, bringing to bear an impressive force of nearly 900 tanks, assault guns and tank destroyers.

On a battlefield where heavy tanks approached a weight of 70 tonnes and even the armour of 30-tonne medium tanks was easily penetrated by the latest anti-tank weapons, relatively light vehicles were surprisingly common. Even as the age of light tanks, so prevalent in the interwar years, began to wane by 1943–44, the armies of the world were not prepared to let go of these inexpensive, reliable and compact chassis. In particular, the Czechoslovak LT vz.38 light tank that served Germany so well in 1939–42 under the designation PzKpfw 38(t) continued its existence as the chassis for the Marder III tank destroyer and 15cm Grille SPG; but while the impressive 7.5cm PaK 40 gun allowed the Marder to fight even the most modern enemy tanks, its thin armour and high profile made it vulnerable to return fire. ČKD engineer Aleksey M. Surin managed to do the impossible, creating a new tank destroyer with a radically lower profile and carrying up to 60mm of highly sloped armour at a weight of 16 tonnes. This thickness of the armour and a powerful 7.5cm PaK 39 gun allowed the Jagdpanzer 38, nicknamed 'Hetzer', to punch above its weight – just the kind of cheap yet powerful AFV the German Army was looking for to replenish its severely depleted armoured force.

A similar tendency could be seen on the other side of the front lines. The Red Army realized the futility of building more two-man T-70 light tanks in 1942, but was not prepared to let go of its well-refined chassis that could be built at automotive factories. Like the Germans, Soviet designers ditched the rotating turret and lengthened the chassis to accommodate a 76mm ZIS-3 field gun and a larger crew. The resulting SPG was designated SU-76, shortly followed by the improved SU-76M. Even though this

This captured Jagdpanzer 38 has been incorporated into a barricade by Polish fighters in Warsaw, 1944. (Hum Images/Alamy Stock Photo)

was intended as a mobile field gun for infantry support, the 10.5-tonne SU-76M could successfully engage even heavy enemy tanks with the right tactics and ammunition.

While Tiger heavy tanks and T-34 medium tanks occupy the spotlight when it comes to the history of armoured warfare, the importance of the light and small Jagdpanzer 38 Hetzer and SU-76M should not be underestimated. This book explores the part they played in the last great tank battle of World War II.

CHRONOLOGY

1939
June — PzKpfw 38(t) production begins in occupied Czechia at BMM.

1942
January — An upgraded version of the PzKpfw 38(t) called the PzKpfw 38(t) nA enters trials, but loses to the PzSpWg II Ausf MAN.
14 February — A prototype of the T-70 is completed.
6 March — T-70 production begins.
May — Work begins on a universal SPG chassis based on T-60 and T-70 components (SU-31 and SU-32).
7 May — Production of the PzKpfw 38(t) ends. All chassis are now used to build tank destroyers or SPGs.
October — Work begins on a new generation of light SPG chassis (SU-11 and SU-12) based on the SU-31.
21 November — SU-12 prototype completed and enters trials.
2 December — SU-12 passes trials and is accepted into production.

1943
7 June — SU-12 (now called SU-76) cancelled due to design defects and its designer is sacked from his post.
9 July — Pilot batch of SU-15Ms is ordered.
21 August — SU-15M officially accepted into service under the designation SU-76M.
October — BMM begins development of a light tank destroyer on the PzKpfw 38(t) nA chassis called leichter Panzerjäger auf 38(t).
6 December — Hitler officially approves the leichter Panzerjäger auf 38(t) project.

1944
January — Designs of the leichter Panzerjäger auf 38(t) are completed and a full-sized model is built.
April — The first three prototypes of the leichter Panzerjäger auf 38(t) are built and mass production of what will come to be called the Hetzer begins.

1945
6 March — German and Hungarian forces execute a counter-offensive near Lake Balaton. Operation *Spring Awakening* begins.

The Hetzer at the Canadian Tank Museum, Oshawa, is technically a G-13, but has been expertly refurbished to depict what it would have looked like if it had been accepted into service in 1945. (Author)

DESIGN AND DEVELOPMENT

SU-76M

Germany's invasion of the Soviet Union forced a serious course correction to the Red Army's light-tank programme. The 14-tonne T-50 promised to bring the same kind of revolutionary leap to the Red Army's light tanks that the T-34 did to its medium tanks, but the machine that entered production in June 1941 was a raw and unrefined design. The Soviet Union, however, could not afford any more time in order to allow the T-50 to go through the growing pains natural for any brand-new vehicle. To make matters worse, a T-50 cost three-quarters as much to build as a T-34 and there were precious few factories with sufficiently powerful lifting equipment to enable them to build the new light tank. Those factories that could build the T-50 were better used to build the T-34 instead.

The Red Army needed a tank that was built on a well-refined and reliable chassis and could be made cheaply. The T-40 small amphibious reconnaissance tank offered the perfect solution. Without the need to swim, it could be built with thicker armour protection, a simpler hull shape and a 20mm automatic cannon instead of a 12.7mm DShK machine gun. This work resulted in the transitional T-30 and then mass production of the T-60 light tank.

The T-60 had no shortage of weaknesses, however, not least of which was that its small 70PS GAZ-202 petrol engine could not offer enough power to drive a vehicle greater than 6 tonnes in weight. The solution was simple: the GAZ-203 power plant

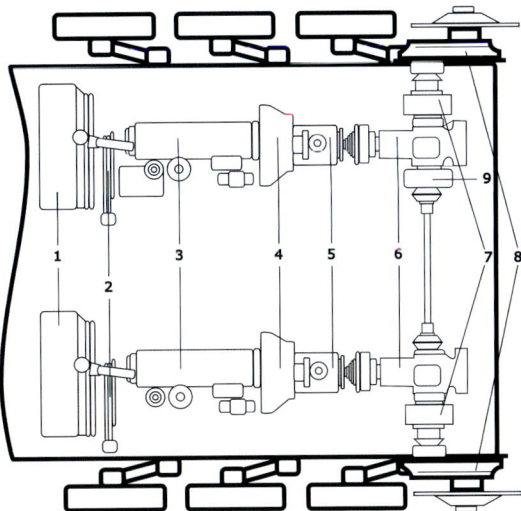

(two GAZ-202s linked together) was installed in a lengthened hull. At 9 tonnes, the new T-70 light tank was half again as heavy as the T-60, but surpassed it in terms of speed, reliability, armour protection and firepower.

The development of a new Soviet light tank with a powerful engine was timely. As Soviet industry pivoted to tank production, the Red Army had to rely on pre-war stocks of prime movers and artillery tractors. The shortage of purpose-made military vehicles was made up for with civilian agricultural tractors pressed into military service. These unarmoured and slow ersatz artillery tractors were better than nothing, but could not keep up with a rapid advance or support the infantry in combat. The solution was simple: the 76mm ZIS-3 divisional gun that made up the core of the Red Army's field artillery could be installed on a purpose-built armoured chassis based on the T-70.

A proposal for an SPG chassis based on components of the T-60 was made as early as 29 January 1942, before the T-70 was in production. The individual behind this project was Semyon A. Ginzburg, an experienced tank designer and one of the highest-ranking figures in the People's Commissariat of Tank Production (NKTP). Ginzburg envisaged that one chassis would be used for carrying a 76mm tank or anti-tank gun; a 37mm anti-aircraft gun, either in a turret or on a rotating mount; a 45mm gun, in which case a turret would be installed instead of a casemate; or no weapon at all, in which case the fighting compartment could be used to transport cargo or infantry. The weight of the completed vehicle would be 7.5–8 tonnes along with a 3.5–4-tonne trailer for additional carrying capacity. To make up for the increased weight, the vehicle would use the same concept of two GAZ-202s arranged in parallel.

Requirements changed soon after Ginzburg submitted his idea, however, and Factory No. 37, the organization in which Ginzburg filled the post of chief designer, was ordered to cease production of the T-60 and begin production of the new T-70. Ginzburg fought against this requirement, as T-60 production had just started after the factory's evacuation from Moscow to Sverdlovsk; retooling to build the T-70 instead would mean all this effort had been wasted.

ABOVE LEFT
T-70 light tank, Patriot Park, Kubinka. The T-70 was based on existing automotive components and could therefore be put into production quickly, easily, and at factories that did not have the necessary equipment to build medium or even light tanks. The same approach was taken to designing an SPG on the T-70's chassis. (Author)

ABOVE RIGHT
Diagram of the SU-12 (SU-76) drivetrain redrawn from the vehicle's manual showing radiators (**1**), ventilation fan drives (**2**), engines (**3**), clutches (**4**), gearboxes (**5**), differentials (**6**), steering clutches (**7**), final drives (**8**) and clutch linkage (**9**). This configuration allowed the reuse of existing automotive components to quickly put a heavier AFV than the T-70 into production, but came with a critical design flaw. (Author)

SEMYON A. GINZBURG

Semyon Aleksandrovich Ginzburg was born on 18 January 1900 in Lugansk, into the family of an ardent revolutionary, so it was no surprise that the young Ginzburg would join the Workers' and Peasants' Red Army in January 1919. His service started in a light-artillery battalion within the 3rd Rifle Division, but after brief courses at the Artillery Command School of the Southern Front he was promoted to lead a light-artillery battery in the 52nd Rifle Division in July 1920. Ginzburg would go on to continue his studies of military science in 1921 at the 4th Kiev Artillery School, then took command courses in Rostov and Krasnodar, finally graduating from the Artillery Academy of the Red Army in Leningrad in 1929. Ginzburg's speciality in this final stage of his studies was not artillery, however, but tanks. The Russian (later Soviet) school grew out of the artillery branch, and Ginzburg was a part of the first wave of tank designers who received a specialized education in the field.

As the tank branch gained prestige, it also gained independence from the artillery branch. The Directorate of Mechanization and Motorization (UMM) was formed in November 1929, and Ginzburg was a natural choice for this new organization, joining it in early 1930. Here, he headed a test group that reviewed the prospective successors to the MS-1 (T-18) light tank. It was Ginzburg who recommended that the British Vickers Mk E light tank be put into production instead of either the T-19 light tank or the T-20 developed in the Soviet Union. Ginzburg was also responsible for adapting the Christie M.1940 light tank into the BT-2 and the Vickers-Carden-Loyd M1931 light amphibious tank into the T-37.

It was not just American and British tank-building experience that Ginzburg helped to integrate into Soviet tank building, but also German. He studied at the Technical Courses of the Osoaviakhim (TEKO), the tank school in Kazan where tankers from Weimar Germany studied and tested their tanks in secret. Ginzburg completed those courses in October 1929, having familiarized himself with many cutting-edge technical solutions implemented in German prototypes. He returned in 1931 to collect a fresh batch of secrets, and as the chief designer of the KB-3 design bureau at the All-Union Arms and Arsenal Conglomerate (VOAO) got to work on integrating them into Soviet production. Under his direction, features of German tanks were incorporated into the T-26 and BT series of tanks. The T-28 medium tank, although an original design, incorporated both the three-turret configuration of the British Vickers Medium Tank Mk III and the suspension from the German Grosstraktor. The same team was responsible for developing the T-35 heavy tank. At the age of only 32, Ginzburg was heavily involved in the creation of an entirely new generation of Soviet tanks. This achievement was rewarded with the Order of Lenin in October 1932.

Ginzburg's design bureau was moved to Leningrad and merged with the Experimental Design and Machinebuilding Department (OKMO) at Factory No. 174. On 1 November 1933, the OKMO was separated into its own organization: Factory No. 185. Here, Ginzburg got to work on designing the next generation of Soviet tanks: the T-46 light tank to replace the T-26; the T-29 medium tank to replace the T-28; the T-26-4 and AT-1 artillery tanks; the SU-5, SU-6 and SU-14 SPGs, as well as several improvements for the tanks that were already in production.

Although almost all of these projects were formally accepted into service, they were only produced in small numbers or not at all. Constantly changing requirements and manufacturing issues undermined the production of a whole generation of Soviet tanks. The timing of this failure was unfortunate, as the Great Terror of 1937–38 ripped through the ranks of Soviet tank designers. Many high-profile figures deemed responsible were executed on the grounds of sabotage, espionage and treason. Although he was arrested on 7 November 1937, Ginzburg could not be connected to any wrongdoing and the charges were dropped.

After he was released, Ginzburg moved to Factory No. 174. In May 1939, he once again rose to the post of Chief Designer. Here, he made another attempt at replacing the T-26. The SP-126 tank incorporated progressive ideas such as the torsion-bar suspension used on the KV-1 heavy tank and the sloped armour of the T-34 medium tank. The SP-126 evolved into the T-50 light tank, which was accepted into service on 16 April 1941. Ginzburg's victory, however, was pyrrhic. There was not enough time to start production of the T-50 and resolve its shortcomings before the German invasion of the Soviet Union. The simpler and lighter T-60 that could be produced in automotive factories was a much better option to replace the Red Army's staggering tank losses.

The demise of another one of Ginzburg's tank types did little to slow down his career. After Factory No. 174 was evacuated to Omsk, Ginzburg moved into the newly formed People's Commissariat of Tank Production (NKTP). As the Deputy Chief of the Technical Department of the NKTP, Ginzburg had more influence on AFV design than ever before. One might have expected him to use his new position to save the T-50, but he saw potential in the chassis of the T-60 as well. Ginzburg oversaw the creation of the SU-31 chassis at Factory No. 37 in Sverdlovsk, turning tried-and-tested components used in the T-60 into a heavier and more powerful chassis capable of carrying a variety of weapons, including a 76mm field gun. After Factory No. 37 was merged with UZTM, Ginzburg continued his work at Factory No. 38, further developing his ideas into the SU-12 SPG. This vehicle was officially accepted into service on 2 December 1942; but what was supposed to be a triumph for Ginzburg turned into a serious failure. The parallel-gearbox layout that worked so well on the SU-31 came with a design defect. Rather than admit and correct his mistake, Ginzburg attempted to shift the blame to subcontractors and assemblers, and interfered with any attempts to correct the root problem in his gearbox design. As reports of breakdowns became more and more frequent and one sticking-plaster solution after another failed to solve the problem, Stalin lost his patience. The SU-12 (designated SU-76 by that point) was removed from production. Ginzburg was fired from his post and prohibited from working on tanks ever again.

Even though he had lost his job, Ginzburg kept his military rank of Engineer-Colonel and received a new post of Technical Deputy Commander in the 32nd Tank Brigade on 17 July 1943. His combat career was brief, however, as he was killed by a bomb blast on 3 August 1943 east of Belgorod during the offensive stage of the battle of Kursk. Engineer-Colonel Semyon Aleksandrovich Ginzburg was buried 300m north of the village of Luchki, Tamarovka District, Kursk Oblast.

Ginzburg managed to save the T-60 for the time being and continued to push for a light SPG chassis based on the T-60, even though the Main Artillery Directorate (GAU) insisted on a chassis based on the T-70. Two vehicles were built: 'chassis 31' or SU-31 that used components of the T-60 tank and 'chassis 32' or SU-32 that used components of the T-70. Even though both vehicles were universal platforms, the SU-31 SPAAG received a 37mm 61-K anti-aircraft gun and the SU-32 SPG a 76mm ZIS-3 field gun. A prototype of the SU-31 was completed in June 1942 and the SU-32 was finished in July. Trials of both vehicles began on 21 August, and even though the SU-31 was based on an inferior tank, it performed better than the SU-32. This was of little consolation to Ginzburg, however, as production of the T-60 at Factory No. 37 ended and the factory became a subsidiary of the Uralmash plant at Yekaterinburg. Its equipment was put to use building components for the T-34 instead of light SPGs.

Despite the demise of the SU-31, Ginzburg was satisfied with the overall concept of the vehicle. Promoted to the post of Chief of the Main Design Department of the NKTP in 1942, he continued to pursue development of a light SPG. This work was now undertaken by the design bureau at Factory No. 38 led by M.N. Schukin, although Ginzburg was still the guiding force behind this design. The resulting chassis was similar to the SU-31, but built with components of the T-70B light tank. Assembly of prototypes was authorized on 19 October 1942 and two vehicles were delivered on 21 November: a SPAAG (SU-11) and an assault gun (SU-12). Both vehicles undertook brief mobility trials and were then sent to the Gorohovets Artillery Proving Grounds for gunnery trials on 5 December, but the trials were only a formality. Orders to prepare for mass production were given on 2 December in State Committee of Defence (GKO) decree #2559, with the SU-12 expected to replace the T-70 in production by the end of the year. Subsequent trials showed that this was the correct decision, as the GAZ-71 SPG built by the Gorky Automotive Factory arrived at the trials late, broke down and had to be disqualified.

The SU-12 was not without its own issues, however. The configuration of two parallel engines and two parallel GAZ-MM gearboxes that worked so well on the SU-31 proved troublesome. The SU-11 suffered a serious breakdown of one gearbox after driving for 350km and had to limp on one engine for the rest of the trials. The same thing happened to the SU-12 after 400km. Ginzburg's spotless reputation and high rank allowed him to argue successfully that the issue lay not in his complex dual-gearbox system, but in poor quality of assembly. Ginzburg personally supervised the assembly of the first SU-12 vehicles and it seemed that the gearbox issue had been corrected when a pilot vehicle drove for 500km in follow-up reliability trials held on 29-31 December 1942 without any breakdowns.

Impressions of the SU-12 from training and front-line units were mixed, however. On one hand, the 76mm gun was a powerful weapon and having a battery of them closely following infantry without fear of getting stuck in mud or having the crew killed by shell splinters was quite useful. On the other hand, technical defects began to manifest themselves. Issues with the dual-gearbox system continued, but they were hidden by other 'growing pains' and it was easy for Ginzburg to deflect responsibility. In addition to assembly at Factory No. 38, Ginzburg blamed GAZ for supplying faulty gearboxes, although the Chief Designer at GAZ, Andrey A. Lipgart, noted that the same gearboxes did not exhibit any problems when used in GAZ-MM trucks.

As Ginzburg suppressed any criticisms of his parallel-gearbox design, Factory No. 38 quietly attempted to fix the problem he had created. Schukin partially mitigated the issue by incorporating a flexible clutch, shock absorbers and a reinforced floorplate. Repair crews from Factory No. 38 were sent to front-line units in order to perform refurbishments in the field. This was only a half-measure, however. Schukin could offer no 'silver bullet' for the gearbox problem and got to work on a completely different SPG with an all-new transmission layout.

SU-11 SPAAG built on the same chassis as the SU-12 SPG (the future SU-76). This vehicle is commonly misidentified as a ZSU-37 SPAAG, but the dual access hatches in the upper front plate are a sign of the earlier experimental vehicle. (Alan Wilson/Wikimedia/CC BY-SA 2.0)

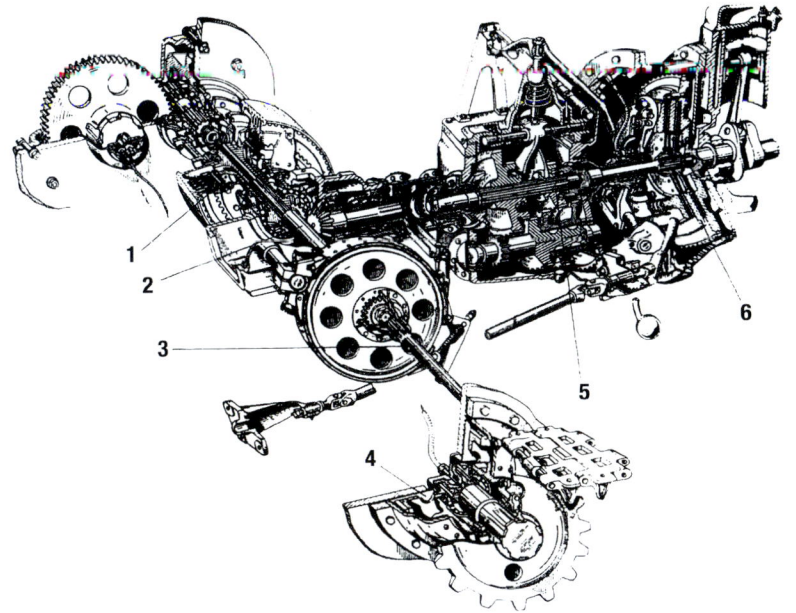

Diagram of the SU-15M (SU-76M) from the vehicle's manual showing the steering clutch (**1**), differential (**2**), left axle (**3**), final drive (**4**), gearbox (**5**) and main clutch (**6**). This layout more closely replicated the transmission used on the T-70B light tank with one gearbox and clutch for both engines. (Author)

This marked the end of Ginzburg's influence on light SPG development. Furious not so much about the technical defects themselves but their cover-up, Stalin sacked Ginzburg from his post on 7 June 1943, prohibiting him from any further involvement in the development of armoured vehicles. The SU-12 (renamed SU-76 in May 1943) was removed from production immediately. Components that were already completed were scrapped rather than being used to build any additional vehicles. People's Commissar of Tank Production Isaac M. Zaltsman and GAU Chief Colonel-General (later Marshal of Artillery) Nikolai D. Yakovlev were chastised by Stalin for allowing this disaster to continue for so long. Both of them kept their heads and their posts, however. Factory No. 38 was spared, as its workers, designers and engineers were shown to have done their best to produce a high-quality vehicle despite Ginzburg's meddling.

Even though he escaped punishment, Schukin still had to deal with the mess his former boss had created. Since the T-70B did not exhibit any issues with its transmission, the new SU-15 SPG copied its transmission layout. Schukin also took the opportunity to introduce improvements to the fighting compartment. The gun trails that took up valuable room inside the vehicle were eliminated. The force from the recoil of the gun was now redirected through the foundation of the gun mounting. Visually, the SU-15 was very similar to the SU-12, but there was only one gearbox maintenance hatch on the front of the vehicle. There was a back-up variant, the SU-38, which used the same casemate on top of the T-70B chassis and therefore had just five road wheels per side instead of six.

The GAU tested the new vehicles very carefully in order to avoid repeating its mistakes. Four of each type of SPG were ordered and built in April 1943 and comparative mobility trials were held in April and May between a T-70B tank, the SU-15, SU-38 and SU-74 (GAZ's competitor in the new tender). The trials revealed defects in the SU-38 and SU-74, but the SU-15 performed well despite being built with refurbished components. Gunnery trials were held in June, in which the SU-15 once again came out on top due to its having a longer chassis than the SU-38, which resulted in greater stability.

Two views of an SU-76M exhibited at Gorky Park, Moscow. This is an example of the late type, which entered production in April 1945. (Stolbovsky/Wikimedia/ CC BY-SA 3.0)

Nevertheless, changes were requested. In order to ensure maximum reliability by reducing the load on the engine, the SU-15's weight had to be reduced, so the vehicle lost the roof it had inherited from the SU-76. Additional weight was saved by reducing the thickness of the rear and side armour to just 25mm at the front and 13–15mm on the sides – enough to protect the SU-15 from bullets and shell splinters but not much else. The resulting vehicle, now designated SU-15M, weighed 10.5 tonnes. A pilot batch of 25 vehicles was ordered on 8 July 1943, but it was already clear which of the three SPG designs would be the winner in the tender. The SU-38 (designated SU-16 after the same changes to its casemate and armour were made) was deemed unsuitable for the 76mm gun due to the reduced length of the vehicle's chassis and smaller fighting compartment; and though work continued on the SU-74, it was clear that GAZ had lost out to Factory No. 38 yet again.

An order for 225 SU-15Ms was placed on 9 July 1943. Trials of the SU-15M prototype and SU-16 were conducted at the Kubinka proving grounds between 10 and 20 August, but it was clear that the SU-15M (now designated SU-76M) was the right choice. In addition to Factory No. 38, GKO decree #3964ss signed on 21 August ordered production of the SU-76M to be undertaken at the GAZ and Factory No. 40. Building this relatively simple vehicle at three factories simultaneously ensured that it would become one of the commonest AFVs in the Red Army. Production ended in October 1945 with 13,679 vehicles having been built.

This was not the end of work on the SU-76M, however. One of the major complaints about the new vehicle was its lack of a roof. Indeed, crews often made their own roofs out of whatever materials they had handy. As Factory No. 38 moved to Kharkov and merged with Factory No. 75 by the summer of 1944, work on an official roof began at Factory No. 40. Tests of the new roof design were held in October 1944. The design bureau led by N.A. Popov added a 4mm-thick roof and extended the sides all the way to the top. The rear portion of the roof was sloped in order to reduce weight. In addition to a commander's periscope and gunsight, two MK-IV periscopes were added to the roof in order to make up for the loss of visibility. This still left the SU-76M fairly blind and introduced another problem: poor ventilation. The concentration of carbon-monoxide fumes in the fighting compartment exceeded the acceptable limits by 50 per cent. There was another option, however. A second prototype was sent to Kubinka that

SU-76M, LAKE BALATON

An SU-76M typical of the late World War II period. The commonest winter camouflage applied to Soviet vehicles at this time was water-soluble whitewash mixed in the field from pre-made mixes or readily available materials such as chalk, plaster and slaked lime. Spring rains would wash off this camouflage and reveal the green underneath, which helped to hide the vehicle in environments with partially melted snow. A tarpaulin protects the crew from rain and snow.

had all the improvements of the first prototype with a roof such as higher sides and new pistol ports that could fit a 7.62mm DT machine gun, but without the roof itself. Only a bar was added across the top of the side plates that could be used to mount the DT to enable it to fire at airborne targets. This vehicle offered much better protection from the sides and rear with no ventilation or visibility problems, and it was only 100kg heavier than the original SU-76M. The so-called 'small modernization' was recommended for production, but the necessary design changes were only implemented by subcontractors by March 1945. Assembly of the new SU-76M began in April. In all, 3,454 SU-76Ms produced between April and October 1945 had the improved side and rear armour. It is unlikely that vehicles of this type reached Germany in time to be used in battle, but many were used in the campaign against Japan in August 1945.

JAGDPANZER 38 HETZER

Disappointed in Škoda's LT vz.35 light tank, the Czechoslovak Army announced a tender for a new tank on 30 October 1937. This time, the winner was Czechoslovakia's other tank-building giant, ČKD. As the company was already dominating foreign markets with a series of excellent light tanks designed by Aleksey Surin, it was not difficult to present a variant modified to fit Czechoslovakian needs. This tank was accepted into service as the LT vz.38.

Unfortunately, Surin's new tank could do precious little to defend his country from Germany. Czechoslovakia's fate was sealed by the Munich Agreement, signed on 30 September 1938, which made it clear that no one was coming to its aid. The Sudetenland came under German control on 30 September 1938 without a single shot being fired. On 15 March 1939 the remainder of Czechoslovakia was cut in two: Czechia was occupied by Germany and Slovakia became a puppet of the Nazi government. The Germans turned out to be quite interested in the LT vz.38. It was slightly more expensive than their own PzKpfw II light tank but its characteristics were closer to those of the PzKpfw III medium tank. Production at ČKD (renamed BMM during the German occupation of Czechoslovakia) continued. The tank went through a number of designations in German service, but quickly settled on the one by which it is best known today: PzKpfw 38(t).

The role of the light tank on the battlefield was changing. As the armour and armament of tanks grew, the gap between the abilities of light tanks and medium tanks grew as well. The primary purpose of a light tank was shifting from infantry support to reconnaissance, and a tender for a new reconnaissance tank was announced on 15 September 1939. German companies had a head start, but constantly changing requirements introduced delays that allowed BMM to catch up. The company's prototype reconnaissance tank, the PzKpfw 38(t) nA (*neuer Art*, new type), was completed in December 1941. Despite being reminiscent of the PzKpfw 38(t), it was heavier, had a reinforced suspension and a more powerful engine, among other upgrades. The Czechoslovak project lost the tender to the Luchs reconnaissance tank, but only 100 Luchs were ever built, while the PzKpfw 38(t) nA waited for its moment.

Initially accepted into service as the LT vz.38, Aleksey M. Surin's tank is better known by its German designation: PzKpfw 38(t). The chassis of this tank was further developed to make a variety of vehicles, the last of which was the Jagdpanzer 38 tank destroyer. (Author)

While the PzKpfw 38(t) had armour and firepower comparable to those of the PzKpfw III in 1939, the Czechoslovak chassis had reached its design limits. Its potential as a gun tank was fully exhausted by 1941, when the Germans encountered the Red Army's powerful new T-34 and KV-1 tanks. Tank destroyers were needed urgently, and so a decision was made to use the PzKpfw 38(t) as a chassis for tank destroyers. The PzSfl 2 was a relatively simple conversion, consisting of a PzKpfw 38(t) tank with a superstructure installed on top of its turret platform. A 7.62cm PaK 36(r) – the Soviet 76.2mm F-22 field gun adapted for German use as an anti-tank gun – with an expanded gun shield was installed in the centre of the superstructure. Expediency was key, and the vehicle that went into production in March 1942 was a product of many compromises. Its high profile and thin armour made it a tempting target on the battlefield, however.

As supplies of captured F-22 field guns would soon be exhausted, work on a vehicle armed with the German 7.5cm PaK 40 anti-tank gun began in parallel. The Sfl 38 – later renamed *7,5 cm PaK 40 auf Pz.Kpfw.38(t)* – had a somewhat improved layout, with a more sensibly designed fighting compartment and gun shield. The third vehicle in the family that entered production in May 1943, the *7,5 cm PaK 43/3 auf Sfl.38 (Ausf.M) Motor vorn* ('7.5cm PaK 43/3 on the 38 self-propelled chassis, variant M, front engine'), offered a much better solution. The components of the chassis were rearranged to carve out as much space as possible, allowing the fighting compartment to be moved back and down. While this reduced the height of the vehicle, it did not solve any other problems. The crew was still protected only by bulletproof armour at the front and sides and by nothing at all at the rear and on top – an uncomfortable fact for a vehicle that was expected to engage enemy tanks as a part of its primary mission.

Not surprisingly, BMM got to work on designing a new tank destroyer by October 1943. This vehicle was designated PzKpfw 38(t)-18 at the factory and *leichter Panzerjäger auf 38(t)* by the Waffenamt Prüfwesen 6 (6th Weapons Testing

ALEKSEY M. SURIN

Aleksey Mikhailovich Surin was born in the village of Polichkovka, in the Bogodukhov District of the Russian Empire, on 10 February 1897. As a son of a rather wealthy landowner, he had no problem obtaining a post-secondary education. Surin studied at the Kiev Polytechnical Institute, but changed the course of his education due to the outbreak of World War I, enrolling at the Officer Artillery Academy in 1916, from which he graduated as a *podporuchik* (second lieutenant). Following the October Revolution in 1917, Surin continued to fight as a member of the White Army, first under Anton I. Denikin, then under Pyotr N. Wrangel. After the Whites were defeated, Surin fled to Turkey, then to Yugoslavia, finally settling in Czechoslovakia where he was able to complete his engineering studies. He graduated from the Faculty of Mechanical and Electrical Engineering at the Czech Technical University in Prague in 1923.

As a part of the Czecho-Moravian Auxiliary Technical Force, Surin made good use of both his military and engineering education. His first project in 1925 was a humble one: adapting a Vickers cannon for production in Czechoslovakia. Surin was drawn into tank building in 1927 when he became involved in the Kolohousenka project, working on the KH-60 light tank (an improvement on the earlier KH-50 light tank). While the KH-60 itself was a failure, it allowed Surin to establish ties with other tank builders. In 1933 he was entrusted with the task of building a dedicated tank department at ČKD, one of Czechoslovakia's leading weapons manufacturers.

Surin's first success came that same year, when the Praha-I (P-I) tankette designed at ČKD was accepted into service with the Czechoslovak Army as the Tančík vz.33 (tankette model 1933). A contract for the production of 50 Praha II (P-II) light tanks was signed with the Czechoslovak Army that same year. This tank was accepted into service as the LT vz.34 (light tank model 1934).

This success was short-lived, however, as the Tančík vz.33 quickly became obsolete and the LT vz.34 turned out to be unsatisfactory in many ways. A new tender was announced. The modernized P-II-a lost to Škoda's Š-II-a light tank, which was accepted into service as the LT vz.35 (light tank model 1935) in the following year.

Surin's career was not particularly set back by this turn of events. A new customer approached ČKD and Škoda: Iran. Surin quickly got to work, adapting the P-I and P-II for the needs of the new Imperial Iranian Army. Surin's new tank was designated the TNH and the tankette the AH-IV. While both vehicles received significant improvements compared with their predecessors, the most important upgrade by far was the suspension. Surin's brand-new suspension (the patent was granted in 1935) resolved one of the biggest issues with the LT vz.34. The suspension used on that tank had been inherited from British Vickers tankettes and turned out to be entirely unsuitable for a heavier vehicle. Surin's new design had four large road wheels per side, coupled together into two bogies of two each. A leaf spring was placed in between, allowing for considerably greater travel than the suspension used on the P-II. The top speed of the TNH increased to 37km/h and the AH-IV's to 40km/h. Prototypes of each design demonstrated in September 1935 impressed the Iranian commission and the order was expanded to 50 TNHs and 50 AH-IVs, which more than made up for the lack of interest expressed by the Czechoslovak Army.

Surin's tanks also piqued the interest of other armies. Sweden purchased 46 AH-IVs in 1937 with the company designation AH-IV-Sv and Strv m/37 in Swedish Army service. These vehicles were designated as light tanks in the Swedish Army and only written off in 1953. Sweden was also interested in the TNH tank. The variant adapted for Swedish use was designated the TNH-Sv and a contract for 90 vehicles was signed in 1939, but those built for Sweden were seized by the Germans and put into service as the PzKpfw 38(t) Ausf S. Because Sweden was an important trading partner for Germany, the Nazis could not afford to upset the Swedes, so permission was given to ČKD to sell a production licence. The TNH-Sv was duly put into production at Scania-Vabis under the Swedish Army designation Strv m/41.

Peru signed a contract for 24 Praha LTP light tanks in 1938, which were similar to the TNH but customized to the Peruvians' needs. These tanks served in the Peruvian Army until 1988 under the name Tanque 39. Lithuania was also interested, but delivery of 21 LTL light tanks was not completed before the country was annexed by the Soviet Union in August 1940. The tanks designed for Lithuania were adapted for Switzerland under the designation LTL-H, and 24 served in the Swiss Army under the name Panzerwagen 39.

By the time the Czechoslovak Army began to judge the LT vz.35 as unsatisfactory, Surin's TNH light tank already had attracted interest from around the world, so it is not surprising that the next tender went to ČKD. The TNH-S variant, 150 of which were ordered, was accepted into Czech service as the LT vz.38; but after the annexation of Czechia in March 1939 all of these fell into German hands. The design stood head and shoulders above Germany's own light tanks, and it was not surprising that the LT vz.38 was accepted into German service as the PzKpfw 38(t). Production continued at ČKD, which changed its name to BMM during the German occupation.

Although Surin remained at the company during the occupation, he showed little love for the Nazis and refused an invitation from Heinz Guderian, Inspector-General of Armoured Troops, to serve as a tank expert in Germany. Although Surin was awarded the Order of the German Eagle in 1944, he faked a 'heart condition' with the help of his brother and used it as an excuse to avoid ever receiving the award. The heart condition was also used as an excuse to avoid punishment when the Germans began looking into his activity on the Jagdpanzer 38 project, on which he had introduced design and manufacturing issues to slow down production. The idea to drill holes in the frontal armour to lighten the load on the suspension, making thus-modified vehicles useless for combat, also belonged to Surin. This obvious act of sabotage later allowed him to escape punishment at the hands of the NKVD.

Alexey Surin helped set up production of the T-34-85 medium tank in Czechoslovakia in the 1950s. After that, he stopped making weapons until his retirement in 1960, although he continued to work for a few years after that as a consultant. He died on 6 April 1974 from a stroke and was buried at the Ďáblický cemetery in Prague.

Surin's contributions to the armoured forces of Sweden earned him the Order of Vasa in 1948. He was also posthumously awarded the Golden Linden Decoration by the Ministry of Defence of the Czech Republic in 2015.

Office), which was supervising development on behalf of the German Army. The PzKpfw 38(t)-18 was supposed to weigh 13 tonnes thanks to a considerable increase in armour thickness, necessitating the use of components originally developed for the PzKpfw 38(t) nA chassis. The same 220PS Praga NRI engine was also envisaged, which would give the vehicle a top speed of 50–60km/h. The rest of the vehicle was clearly inspired by the Jagdpanzer IV tank destroyer, as sloped plates of armour of a very similar shape were used. The 7.5cm PaK 39 main gun was the same as on the Jagdpanzer IV and elements of the gun mount and gun mantlet were similar.

Owing to this reuse of components and ideas, development of the PzKpfw 38(t)-18 was rapid. The first full-sized model was completed on 24 January 1944, just 1½ months after Hitler approved the project. The first three prototypes were due in April, which was also when production was scheduled to begin. Of course, such a rushed schedule introduced problems. For one, the Praga NRI engine was not ready in time and the weaker 160PS Praga AE petrol engine had to be used; and instead of the expected 13 tonnes, the vehicle – now called 7.5cm Panzerjäger 38(t) – weighed in at 16 tonnes. This weight gain not only further reduced the power-to-weight ratio and therefore the vehicle's mobility, but also overloaded the front wheels. This problem was only discovered during trials of the three prototypes built in April, meaning that the first 20 production vehicles all had this drawback. It was resolved in radical fashion by drilling holes in the front plate to lighten the load and covering them up with 5mm-thick armour. Naturally, this disqualified the first 20 vehicles from front-line service.

Another radical attempt to lighten the load on the front wheels included removing the recoil buffer and installing the gun rigidly. This solution reduced the weight of the vehicle by almost 1 tonne and freed up space to carry 41 additional rounds of ammunition, more than doubling the vehicle's stowage capacity. The power-to-weight ratio was further improved by using the 180PS Typ 928 diesel engine. This variant of the vehicle was designated Jagdpanzer 38 Starr; but while the first prototype was converted in April 1944, development was slow. Another prototype was converted in May, two more in September, and although production of a ten-unit pilot batch began at Škoda in December 1944 the last vehicle was not finished until April 1945. It turned out that the lack of recoil buffers damaged both the gun and the vehicle itself when firing, and so the Jagdpanzer 38 Starr was only used for training.

Smaller design changes to reduce the load on the front suspension as well as adapt the tow hooks and lifting eyes for the extra weight were also urgently introduced. Five iterations of the gun mounting were introduced in 1944 alone, each shaving off precious weight. The plates in the front leaf springs were thickened from 7mm to 9mm after September 1944, as complaints came in from front-line units that they were prone to breakages. The number of bolts holding the road wheels was also increased to 32. A new observation device was introduced in September, as it turned out that the old one was easily destroyed when shells hit the frontal armour and ricocheted. The manner in which the muffler was attached was also changed in November. This change was accompanied by a new name for the vehicle – Jagdpanzer 38 – which was the name that stuck. Some front-line troops nicknamed it 'Hetzer', but this name was never officially used.

All these changes did no favours to BMM, which struggled to keep up with demand. While production quotas for April, May and June 1944 were met, output in July was 100 units below quota. The discrepancy grew, resulting in a delivery of just 1,267 Jagdpanzer 38s in 1944 against a stated quota of 2,073. Out of 1,350 Jagdpanzer 38s due in the first quarter of 1945, BMM delivered only 710. The quota was lowered to 350 vehicles per month starting in April, but even this goal was a pipe dream as only 70 were actually delivered.

Škoda was likewise behind schedule, struggling to deliver even half of its quota and producing just 310 out of an envisaged 810 Jagdpanzers by the end of the year. Even though Škoda was expected to catch up with BMM's production quota by January 1945, it could not match even BMM's actual rate of production, let alone the expected numbers. Only 423 Jagdpanzer 38s were delivered in the first quarter of 1945 and 47 more in April.

On 26 September 1944, the OKH decided to begin production of the Jagdpanzer 38 at Alkett in Berlin. This move was made largely out of desperation, as the Allied strategic bombing campaign continued to deplete the Nazi regime's industrial resources at a time when it needed AFVs more than ever. A total of 1,000 vehicles per month were needed from Alkett, but the company's highest monthly output of StuG assault guns was just 500 units. Furthermore, the StuG was also about to lose its chassis, as the ever-worsening situation on every operational front forced the Germans to rationalize their production to just three types of tanks. The new streamlined German armoured forces would use the Tiger Ausf B as their heavy tank and the Panther as their medium tank, with the only option for a light chassis being the Jagdpanzer 38. The chassis was not without its drawbacks, but it had similar armament and armour to the much heavier and more expensive StuG and pursuing any other option would simply take too long to deliver.

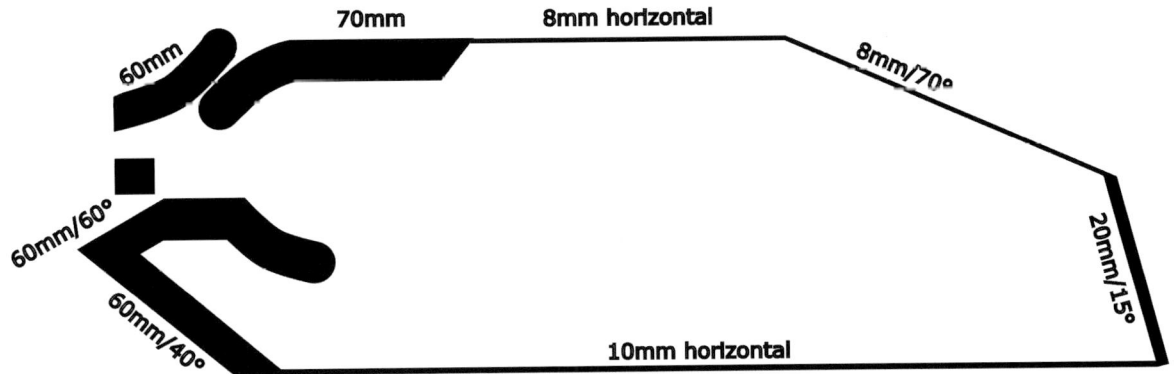

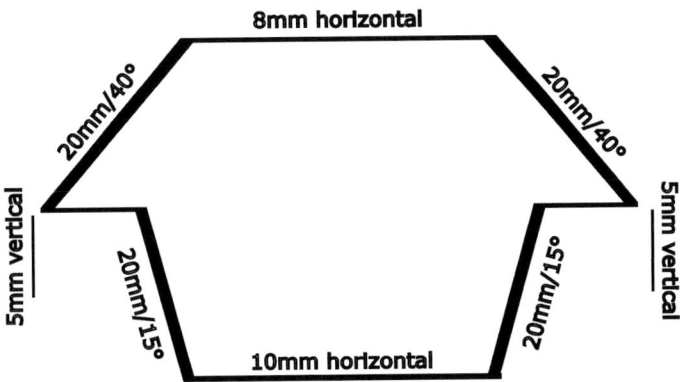

Armour diagram showing the contrast between the Hetzer's frontal protection and other parts of the hull. The mass of armour concentrated at the front made the vehicle unbalanced, shifting excess pressure on to the front wheels. (Author)

Unfortunately, the Jagdpanzer 38 was considered to be unsuitable for production in Germany, so Alkett got to work converting the design to suit the abilities of their equipment, making improvements along the way. Alkett's new tank destroyer was called the Jagdpanzer 38D. The Praga AE made way for a 220PS Tatra 103 diesel engine, combined with the ZF AK 5-80 gearbox. This would increase the top speed of the tank destroyer to 40km/h. The lower hull sides were no longer sloped but vertical, which allowed wider track links to be used. Enough room was freed up to install a volute spring suspension, which was strong enough to support 20 tonnes of weight. In addition to the 7.5cm PaK 39 gun, the Jagdpanzer 38D would be able to carry a 7.5cm PaK 42 L/70 gun or a 10.5cm Sturmhaubitze 42/2 howitzer. As Germany's only light chassis, the vehicle could also be built as the Aufklärer 38D reconnaissance tank with an open-top turret carrying a 20mm autocannon or a 75mm gun; the Bergepanzer 38D ARV; the Kugelblitz 38D SPAAG; an armoured personnel carrier; or a carrier for a 120mm mortar.

Production of the Jagdpanzer 38D was scheduled to begin at Alkett in January 1945, where it was expected to reach 800 units per month by the end of the year. It was envisaged that VOMAG would join Alkett in June and produce an additional 300 vehicles per month by December. Aufklärer 38D production was scheduled to begin at MIAG starting in January 1945 and was also expected to reach 300 units per month. BMM was also supposed to transition to production of the Jagdpanzer 38D

The Hetzer at the Musée des Blindés, Saumur. The new tank destroyer was much better protected than its predecessor, but this came at the cost of a weight increase of 50 per cent. (Author)

design, starting in September 1945. In reality, very little was ready before the end of the war. It is known that Zahnradfabrik sent gearboxes to Alkett on 5 April and that two Jagdpanzer 38D prototypes were due by the end of that month. As the Red Army entered Spandau on 27 April, however, all the work was for naught. If any prototypes were completed, they were likely mistaken for regular Jagdpanzer 38s and scrapped. Alkett's documentation was lost in a fire, shrouding the fate of the Jagdpanzer 38D in mystery.

Despite these shortfalls in production, the Jagdpanzer 38 was built in large numbers: 2,827 were completed in total, of which 2,612 were built as the basic type, 14 more (ten production and four prototypes) as the Jagdpanzer 38 Starr with a rigidly mounted gun, 20 as the Flammpanzer 38 flamethrower tank and 181 as the Bergepanzer 38 ARV.

Škoda ended the war with 1,200 Jagdpanzer 38s on hand, but there was only enough armament available to equip 78 of them. A number of these tank destroyers were completed after the war and designated G-13 after the factory code used at Škoda (G = SPG, 1 = light weight class, 3 = third vehicle). Almost all the Jagdpanzer 38s displayed in museums today are actually G-13s that only left the Škoda factory after the war.

HETZER, LAKE BALATON

A Hetzer used by the Hungarian forces at Lake Balaton. Obscured here, Hungarian Army tactical markings were applied over the German markings when the vehicles were received. The prefix 'T' indicated that this Hetzer belonged to the 20th Assault Artillery Battalion. Since the Hetzer's primary defence was not being seen in the first place, the vehicle was covered in branches to help it blend in with the terrain.

THE STRATEGIC SITUATION

The Red Army conducted ten major offensive operations against Nazi Germany in 1944 that came to be known as Stalin's Ten Blows, each of which significantly undermined the German positions on the Soviet–German Front. Stalin's Ninth Blow was aimed at eliminating one of Germany's few remaining allies: Hungary. The 2nd, 3rd and 4th Ukrainian fronts struck from West Ukraine, Bulgaria and Romania, capturing a number of key cities and encircling Budapest. Oilfields at Bükkszék and Nagykanizsa were now in Soviet hands. These oilfields contributed a significant portion of fuel available to Germany, and their loss severely undermined its ability to stay in the war. To make matters worse the Soviet, Bulgarian and Yugoslavian armies were now free to strike at Czechoslovakia and Austria from north-west of Budapest. This would result not only in the loss of the oilfields at Zistersdorf and critical industrial regions, but also form a staging ground for a follow-up attack against southern Germany. Even at the height of its power, however, the Red Army could not carry out a strategic offensive of this scope immediately after advancing as far as 250km over the course of seven weeks. The Soviets had to stop, refuel and refit. Even though German forces were giving ground on every front, they could not allow such an opportunity to go to waste. The counter-attack had to be delivered here and now.

The first counter-attacks were delivered in January 1945 and targeted the 4th Guards Army of the 3rd Ukrainian Front. The Soviet formation was exhausted after weeks of fighting, and to make things worse the German counter-attack was mistakenly expected on 3 January, and even then in the wrong place. The attacking

A Hetzer and German crewmen in East Prussia. The terrain is muddy and would be difficult for the Hetzer to traverse due to the narrow width of its tracks for its weight. (Scherl/Süddeutsche Zeitung Photo/Alamy Stock Photo)

force, consisting of the IV. SS-Panzerkorps and elements of the 6. Armee (seven tank and two motorized divisions in total), struck against the 31st Rifle Corps north-west of Budapest on 2 January. The Soviet defences established there were shallow, and specialized anti-tank units were absent completely. Only general-purpose divisional artillery was available to combat German heavy tanks in the first few days. German forces penetrated Soviet defences to a depth of 27–31km, reaching Tát and Esztergom. There was a serious risk of a breakthrough to the besieged Hungarian capital, but Soviet deployment of specialized anti-tank artillery units and ground-attack aircraft from the 17th Air Army brought the Panzers to a halt.

A second Axis attempt to break through to Budapest was undertaken on 7 January north of Székesfehérvár, towards Zámoly. This time, the defending 20th Rifle Corps was ready for the German tanks, and the attack only penetrated to a depth of 4–5km before petering out.

The Germans seemingly gave up. Soviet scouts reported that German tank columns were pulling out of Esztergom and Bicske. Prisoner interrogations revealed that the German forces were being reallocated to reinforce Heeresgruppe Mitte and the Western Front. This, of course, was a ruse. The Germans gathered five armoured divisions to strike at the 4th Guards Army once more, this time between lakes Balaton and Velence. This attack began on 18 January and progressed much more successfully than the first two. The 135th Rifle Corps forming the first line of defence was pushed behind the Sárvíz River and by 20 January the Germans had reached the Danube. The 3rd Ukrainian Front was cut in two, Székesfehérvár was under threat of encirclement, and there was a serious danger that the Germans would turn north, breaking the siege of Budapest. Even this offensive was not long-lived, however. Attempts to break through to Budapest that began on 22 January failed, and even though the Germans managed to retake Székesfehérvár, the 4th Guards Army carried out an orderly retreat, avoiding encirclement. A new stable line of defence was established between Zámoly and the Danube.

In the meantime, elements of the 3rd Ukrainian Front continued to chip away at the defences in Budapest. Pest (the part of the city east of the Danube) was declared indefensible on 17 January and its garrison was withdrawn west to defend Buda (the western part of the city). The 3rd Ukrainian Front began its assault on Buda on 20 January. German and Hungarian forces defended the city fiercely, but as attempts to relieve them failed it was only a matter of time before the Hungarian capital would fall. Even though Hitler declared Budapest a *Festung* (fortress city) to be defended to the last man, half of the city's defenders attempted a breakout westwards on the night of 11/12 February. Only 785 men without heavy *matériel* made it to the German lines. The rest of the defenders were either killed or taken prisoner by the end of the day on 13 February.

There was no longer an urgent need to advance on this axis with the loss of the Budapest garrison, but the salient formed by the successful advance against the 4th Guards Army made for a good launch pad for a follow-up offensive. Operation *Spring Awakening* aimed to slash the 3rd Ukrainian Front in half once again, destroying its core and allowing German armoured spearheads to manoeuvre freely in the Soviet rear, turning north against the 2nd Ukrainian Front and breaking into Czechoslovakia. Three axes of attack were planned: the main axis lay between lakes Balaton and Velence, but German forces also planned to circle around the south of Lake Balaton. A third strike would be delivered by Heeresgruppe E across the Drava River, attacking the flank of the 3rd Ukrainian Front held by less-experienced Bulgarian and Yugoslavian forces. This operation, if executed correctly, would return Hungarian oilfields to German control, bolster the wavering resolve of Hitler's Hungarian allies and severely degrade the position of the Red Army on the Soviet–German Front.

Considerable forces were gathered to carry out this offensive. The 6. SS-Panzerarmee was brought over from the Western Front in great secrecy. At the start of the offensive, it consisted of the I. and II. SS-Panzerkorps, I. Kavalleriekorps, 23. Panzer-Division and 44. *Reichsgrenadier* Division. The 6. SS-Panzerarmee's north-eastern flank was held by Armeegruppe Balck, consisting of the 1. and 3. Panzer-Divisionen as well as the 356. Infanterie-Division. Two Tiger II-equipped battalions (schwere SS-Panzer-Abteilung 501 and schwere Panzer-Abteilung 509) were also allocated for the offensive, numbering 66 Tiger IIs operational and 23 tanks undergoing repairs. The German heavy-tank force was further augmented by 31 Tiger IIs from the schwere Panzer-Abteilung *Feldherrnhalle* and a company of eight Tiger tanks from the 3. SS-Panzer-Division *Totenkopf*. These units were reinforced with men as well as *matériel*: three waves of replacement soldiers arrived in March from the Kriegsmarine, Reichsarbeitsdienst and police personnel, totalling 9,000–10,000 men.

The German tank force was augmented by a considerable number of SPGs. In addition to six Jagdpanther tank destroyers from schwere Panzerjäger-Abteilung 560, 30 StuG and StuH assault guns in Sturmgeschütz-Brigade 303 and 25 in

OPPOSITE

This map shows the location of units equipped with Hetzers and SU-76M as of 5 March 1945. Numbers shown indicate functional vehicles at the start of Operation *Spring Awakening*. Most of the Hetzers that were prepared for the attack in between lakes Balaton and Velence were attached to the I. Kavalleriekorps directed towards Enying. By contrast, Soviet SU-76Ms were scattered throughout the front. Even as many light SPG regiments and battalions were battered during the fighting in February, SU-76Ms remained a significant proportion of Soviet armour in this sector.

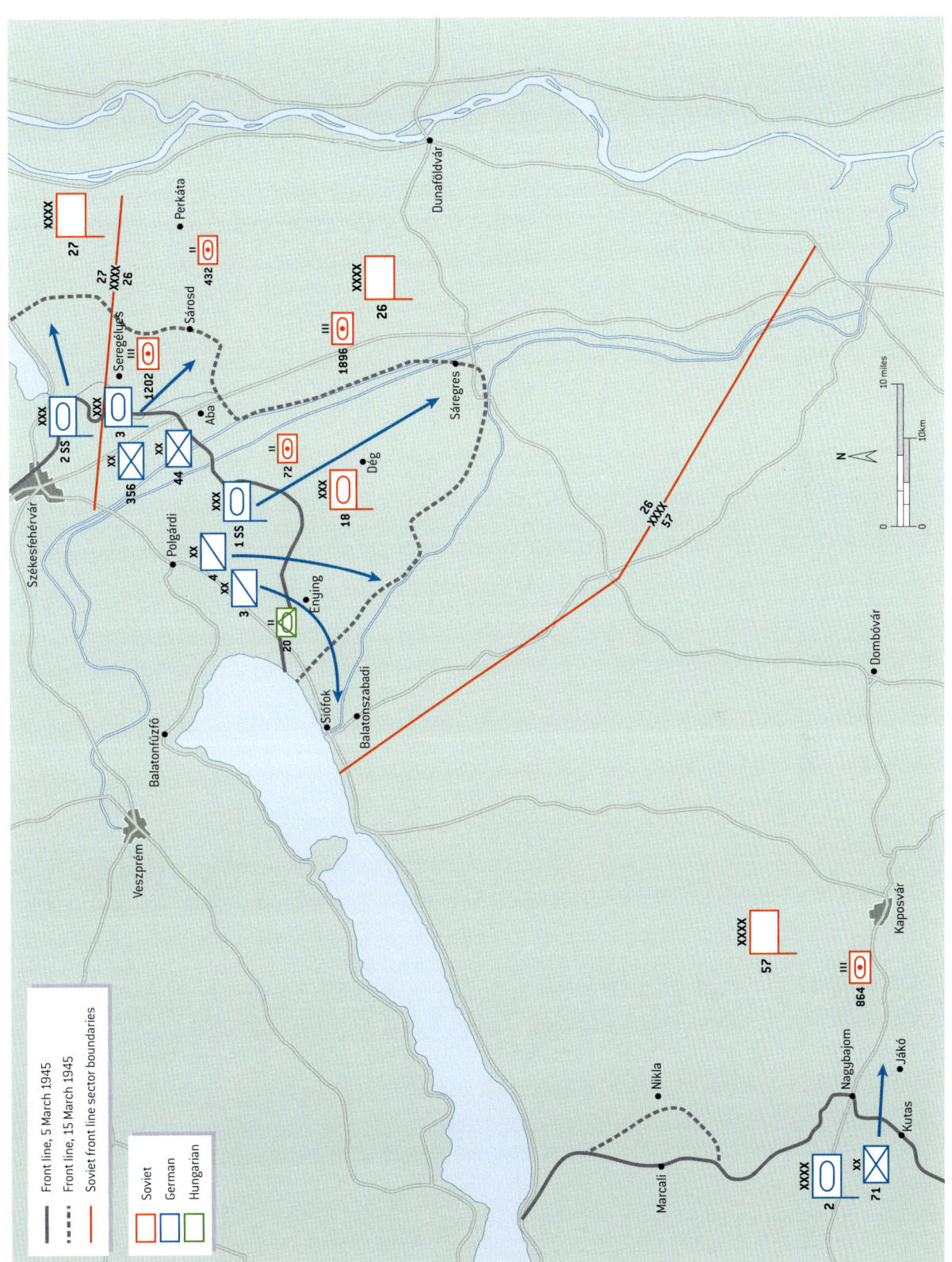

Sturmgeschütz-Brigade 261, German infantry and grenadier divisions included tank-destroyer companies.

In total, Heeresgruppe Süd (Army Group South) could bring a force of 812 tanks and tank destroyers to bear, the bulk of which (679 vehicles) were directed into the narrow opening between lakes Balaton and Velence. A further 167 tanks and 99 SPGs were undergoing repairs and would become available during the battle. Heeresgruppe Süd gathered all it could for one final blow. Luckily for the Red Army, the Germans tipped their hand with a relatively small localized attack carried out in the north, near Esztergom, on 17 February. This attack involved elements of the 6. SS-Panzerarmee and informed the Red Army that there was a new major tank force in theatre. The Soviet *Stavka* (High Command) realized the grave implications of this discovery. As of 20 February, every intelligence asset at Soviet disposal was activated to discover enemy plans. The 3rd Ukrainian Front was instructed to build an echeloned anti-tank defence. The 1st Guards, 26th, 57th and 1st Bulgarian armies made up the first echelon of defence. The 27th Army formed a second echelon. As the Germans were not ones to gather an armoured spearhead long in advance of an attack, an offensive was expected by the Soviets either in late February or early March.

A powerful Soviet armoured force was collected to meet the German attack. Between the 18th and 23rd Tank corps, 1st Guards Mechanized Corps, 5th Guards Cavalry Corps, 208th Self-Propelled Artillery Brigade and 366th Guards Self-Propelled Artillery Regiment, there were 265 tanks and SPGs subordinate directly to the 3rd Ukrainian Front. These consisted of four IS-2 heavy tanks, 34 ISU-122 and ISU-152 heavy SPGs (which could act as tank destroyers at a pinch), 80 of the brand-new SU-100 tank destroyers, 75 T-34 and T-34-85 medium tanks and 51 foreign tanks (chiefly M4A2 Shermans), as well as 23 SU-76 SPGs.

The SU-76 was much more prevalent among the 3rd Ukrainian Front's subordinate infantry formations. The 4th Guards Army had 28 of its own SU-76s, the 26th Army had 16 SU-76s and the 27th Army had seven SU-76s and one T-70 (often used as a commander's tank in SU-76 units). The 57th Army had a truly lavish armoured force in comparison, numbering 21 SU-76s and 67 T-34 or T-34-85 tanks. An after-action study conducted by Lieutenant General Aleksandr P. Tarasov, operations chief of the 3rd Ukrainian Front, credited this to the fact that the 57th Army was the only one out of all the composite armies of the 3rd Ukrainian Front to be defending a relatively quiet portion of the Front, while the others had been fighting constantly since December 1944.

In total, the 3rd Ukrainian Front was in possession of 408 tanks and SPGs, nine of which were undergoing repairs. The SU-76s made up nearly a quarter of the Front's armour with 95 vehicles in total. Even though these were light SPGs intended for infantry support, they would have to do their part when it came to fighting enemy tanks. Instructions were conveyed to hold fire until enemy tanks were within 200–500m, thus ensuring that the 76mm ZIS-3 gun could score a killing blow even against heavy armour.

This was not going to be an easy fight. Soviet intelligence estimated that in the area between lakes Balaton and Velence, the Germans enjoyed a five-fold advantage in armour, a two-fold advantage in artillery and could field 2.3 times as many men

Serving as a mechanized field gun, the SU-76M was rarely apart from supporting infantry. Outside of battle, soldiers could hitch a ride on its armour. (INTERFOTO/History/Alamy Stock Photo)

as the Red Army had in this sector. Tarasov's report noted that this was the largest single group of armour assembled by the Germans during the entire Great Patriotic War (1941–45). The number of German armoured divisions was greater than either of the two pincers employed at Kursk individually, and were gathered on a narrower front line.

The Soviets made up for the shortage of tanks with static defences. Including the second echelon, the Soviet defenders were in possession of 25 anti-tank artillery regiments, plus 25 general-purpose artillery regiments as well as four artillery brigades of the Supreme Command Reserve, bringing the total number of guns and howitzers capable of fighting tanks to 2,976. In addition, 700–750 anti-tank mines and 600–700 anti-personnel mines were laid for each kilometre of the front lines by 5 March. The density of the minefields increased to 2,500–2,700 per kilometre in key directions to a depth of as much as 10–15km. Specially trained mobile sapper units were assembled to carry out so-called 'close quarters' or 'daring' mining missions, which consisted of laying down additional minefields right under the enemy's nose as the battle progressed: 24,500 anti-tank mines, 9,000 anti-personnel mines and 8,700kg of explosives were reserved for this task.

With over 1,000 AFVs and thousands of guns gathered around lakes Balaton and Velence, the stage was set for the last great tank battle of World War II.

TECHNICAL SPECIFICATIONS

LAYOUT AND ARMOUR

The SU-76M consisted of a fixed casemate on top of a chassis made from T-70B light-tank components. The hull was split into four compartments: the driver's compartment in the front, the transmission and engine compartments to his right, and the fighting compartment in the rear. The fighting compartment contained the 76mm ZIS-3 gun, three crewmen and ammunition. If necessary, crewmen could move between the driver's compartment and the fighting compartment through a hatch below the gun.

The armour of the SU-76M was light, offering protection from small arms and heavy machine guns. The upper front plate was 25mm thick, angled at 60 degrees. A cut-out was made in the centre of the plate for a driver's hatch. The curved hatch door, also 25mm thick, had an opening on the top side for a rotating periscope. A portion of the upper front plate could be removed to access the transmission. The lower front plate was 30mm thick, angled at 30 degrees. It contained an opening for the crank starter, protected by an armoured panel when not in use. The floor and roof of the hull were 7mm thick and completely horizontal, with the exception of a small portion of the front floor sloped at 9 degrees. The roof was made in sections and could be removed to service the engine. The sides of the hull were 15mm thick and vertical. The hull rear consisted of two 15mm-thick plates, the top one being vertical and the lower one sloped at 30 degrees. A door was cut into the rear plate for the crew to enter and exit the fighting compartment. Air from the engine compartment exited the vehicle through a grille on the right side.

SU-76M on display at Gorky Park. The frontal armour of the SU-76M was not very thick or highly angled and offered protection from, at best, heavy machine guns and light anti-tank guns. The side and rear armour offered reliable protection only from bullets and shell splinters. (Author)

The casemate protected the gun crew from the front and sides. The frontal armour was 25mm thick, sloped at 25 degrees. The sides of the casemate were 10mm thick, sloped at 20 degrees. An opening for the ZIS-3 gun was cut into the middle, shifted left of the vehicle's centre. Pistol ports were cut into the sides of the casemate, covered by armoured shutters when not in use, and there was a vision port on the left side. An opening for a radio antenna, protected by an armoured cup, was cut into the right side.

A knocked-out SU-76M in Berlin, 1945. (Imwar/Alamy Stock Photo)

The ZIS-3 gun was installed in the gun port on the casemate. The gun's recoil mechanism was protected by an armoured cover 10mm thick in the front and 7mm thick elsewhere. The roof above the gun was also 10mm thick. A 15mm gun mantlet covered the gun port.

The Jagdpanzer 38 was a fully enclosed tank destroyer based on the chassis of the PzKpfw 38(t) nA reconnaissance tank. Unlike earlier tank destroyers built on Czechoslovak chassis, there was no distinct casemate or turret platform. Instead, the vehicle's hull was composed of a series of sloped armoured plates arranged in the shape of two irregular truncated pyramids joined at the base with a large blister in the front for the gun mounting.

The frontal armour plate was 60mm thick and sloped at 60 degrees. A cut-out was made to the right of centre for the gun port, which was protected by a 70mm-thick cast blister and a 60mm-thick cast gun mantlet. An opening was also cut on the left side for the driver's vision slit. The lower front plate was also 60mm thick, sloped at 40 degrees.

The sides of the hull were 20mm thick, sloped at 40 degrees. The lower sides of the hull were also 20mm thick, but sloped at 15 degrees. The rear was likewise 20mm thick and angled at 15 degrees. An 8mm horizontal plate formed the pannier floor. The floor of the hull was 10mm thick.

The hull narrowed at the engine compartment. The roof also sloped downwards at an angle of 70 degrees. This sloping part of the roof was split up into sections, which could be opened to access the engine. The horizontal part of the roof contained an opening for the gunsight as well as two hatches for the crew. Both the sloped and unsloped parts of the roof were 8mm thick.

G-13 at the Deutsches Panzermuseum Munster. A departure from how earlier tank destroyers were built at BMM, the Hetzer was protected from all sides with highly sloped armour. (Author)

G-13 at the Canadian Tank Museum. Even the lower sides of the hull were sloped. This improved protection, but further decreased the amount of space inside the hull. (Author)

WEAPONS

The main weapon of the SU-76M was the 76mm ZIS-3 gun. It was largely identical to the towed divisional gun, but the lower mount and gun trails were removed. Instead, the gun was installed on a beam running across the fighting compartment. This gun mount allowed for -5 degrees of depression, +15 degrees of elevation, and 15 degrees of traverse to either side. A total of 60 rounds of ammunition were carried for this gun: seven on the right side in the back of the fighting compartment stored vertically, 29 to the left of the gun stored horizontally, 17 on the left side in the back stored vertically and seven more on the right side of the gun.

Auxiliary armament consisted of a 7.62mm DT machine gun, which could be fired out of the vehicle's pistol ports; 15 63-round magazines were carried for the DT, for a total of 945 rounds. The DT was stowed on the left side of the fighting compartment when not in use. The crew also had a 7.62mm PPSh-41 submachine gun with six

SU-76M MAIN ARMAMENT

1. Pistol port
2. MK-4 observation periscope
3. Aiming flywheels
4. PG-1M panoramic gunsight
5. Hand trigger
6. Direct vision port
7. TR-4 fire-correction periscope
8. Radio set
9. PPSh-41 submachine gun
10. Ammunition ready rack
11. Reserve ammunition rack
12. Pedal trigger

The 76mm ZIS-3 gun as used in the SU-76M. Introduced in 1941 to replace the larger and heavier F-22-USV, the ZIS-3 was the backbone of Soviet divisional artillery. It was a multi-purpose weapon, capable of functioning both as a field gun and as an anti-tank gun. A variety of ammunition types including HE, canister shot, HEAT and illumination flares developed for Soviet 76mm field guns could be used by the SU-76M as well. While the SU-76M's primary purpose was close support of infantry units, it could also fight enemy tanks with AP shells and APCR shot if the situation demanded it.

HETZER MAIN ARMAMENT

1. SfI ZF1a gunsight
2. 7.5cm PaK 39 gun breech
3. Ammunition ready rack
4. Recoil guard
5. Reserve ammunition
6. Aiming flywheels
7. Trigger
8. Transmission
9. Driver's controls
10. Instrument panel
11. Driver's vision periscopes
12. Brow pad

The 7.5cm PaK 39 gun as used in the Jagdpanzer 38. This was a powerful anti-tank weapon that was a threat to any AFV deployed by the Red Army, but it was also bulky which made it difficult to operate in the vehicle's confined fighting compartment. The 7.5cm PaK 39 was optimized for anti-tank performance, but the Hetzer was often put to use supporting attacking infantry as well.

This 76mm ZIS-3 divisional gun is displayed at Oorlogsmuseum Overloon. The ZIS-3 was a dual-purpose weapon used as a field gun by the Red Army's artillery units but also as an anti-tank gun by tank-destroyer regiments. The SU-76 and SU-76M SPGs carried the same weapon. (Author)

These 76mm OF-350 HE-Fragmentation rounds are stored at the rear of the SU-76M's fighting compartment. The SU-76M fired a heavier HE shell with more explosive filler, generating more lethal fragments and dispersing them over a wider area than the Hetzer's 7.5cm Sprenggranate 34. (Author)

71-round drum magazines (426 rounds) and ten F-1 anti-personnel grenades for close defence. The PPSh-41 was stowed on the right side of the fighting compartment when not in use and the grenades were stored under the bench that the gunner and loader sat on during travel.

The primary weapon of the Jagdpanzer 38 was the 7.5cm PaK 39 L/48 gun. The gun mounting allowed for -6 degrees of depression and +10 degrees of elevation. Traverse was asymmetrical: 11 degrees to the right and 5 degrees to the left. A total of 41 rounds of ammunition were carried for this gun: one box of nine on the left side, ten in the right-side pannier, and 22 in a rack underneath the gun.

A 7.92mm MG 34 machine gun was installed in a mount on the roof as a secondary weapon. This mount had a traverse of 360 degrees and the MG 34 could be fired from inside the vehicle. A gun shield was provided for when a crewman fired it while peeking out of his hatch. A total of 1,200 rounds of ammunition in 24 50-round belts were carried. A 7.92mm Sturmgewehr 43 assault rifle with 180 rounds of ammunition and 20 *Eihandgranate* hand grenades was carried for self-defence.

SU-76M AND HETZER AMMUNITION

The SU-76M fired the BR-350 76mm armour-piercing shell (**1**), weighing 6.5kg fitted in a fixed UBR-353 round. This was the standard armour-piercing round fired by towed and mechanized 76mm divisional guns in Soviet service. The SU-76M's ZIS-3 gun fired this shell at a muzzle velocity of 670m/sec, giving a maximum penetration of 91mm of armour (British standard of 50 per cent chance of perforation, homogeneous armour, angled at 30 degrees). The BR-350 allowed the SU-76M to fight German medium tanks effectively, but heavy tanks could only be defeated at close range by firing at the thinner side armour.

The SU-76M also used the OF-350 high-explosive fragmentation shell (**2**), weighing 6.2kg in a fixed UOF-353 round. This was the standard high-explosive round fired by towed and mechanized 76mm divisional guns in Soviet service. With 710g of high-explosive filler, this was a potent weapon against enemy infantry, light fortifications and even lightly armoured vehicles.

The armour-piercing projectile used by the Hetzer tank destroyer was the 7.5cm Pzgr 39 APCBC shell (**3**) weighing 6.8kg in a fixed 7.5cm PzgrPatr 39 PaK 39 round. Fired at a muzzle velocity of 750m/sec, this shell penetrated up to 102mm of armour (British standard of 50 per cent chance of perforation, homogeneous armour, angled at 30 degrees), enough to damage all but the most heavily armoured Allied tanks.

Weighing 5.74kg in a fixed 7.5cm SprgrPatr 34 Pak 39 round, the 7.5cm Sprgr 34 high-explosive fragmentation shell (**4**) was also used. Despite being designed as a tank destroyer, the Hetzer was often employed as an assault gun in an infantry-support role, where this shell came in handy against enemy infantry and light fortifications.

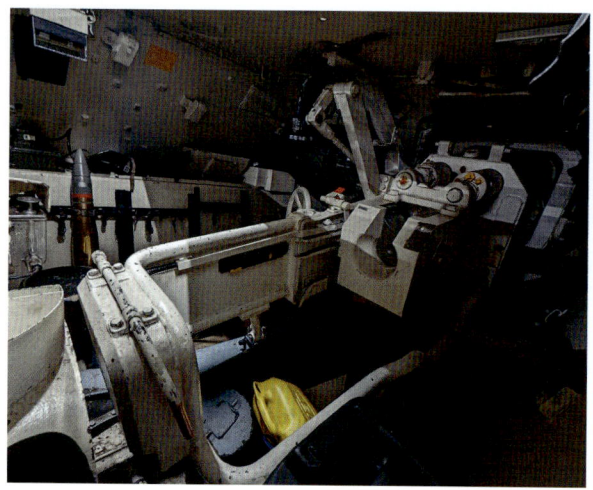 

ABOVE LEFT
The Hetzer's 7.5cm PaK 39 L/48 gun as viewed from the commander's station. (Author)

ABOVE RIGHT
These 7.5cm Pzgr 39 AP rounds are stored on the right side of the Hetzer's fighting compartment. The Hetzer fired a heavier and faster AP shell than the SU-76M, resulting in superior armour penetration. (Author)

The Jagdpanzer 38 was the clear winner in the balance between armour and armament. The SU-76M's armour was light and designed to withstand only machine-gun fire and shell splinters, while as a tank destroyer the Jagdpanzer 38 received armour thick enough to withstand hits from tank guns and armament to match. The 7.5cm PaK 39 L/48 firing a 6.8kg shell at a muzzle velocity of 750m/sec could penetrate 102mm of armour (British standard of 50 per cent chance of perforation, homogeneous armour, angled at 30 degrees). The most effective armour of the SU-76M was 25mm thick at 60 degrees, giving a line-of-sight thickness of 50mm. The Jagdpanzer 38's gun could defeat that armour at any range.

The SU-76M's ZIS-3 gun fired a 6.5kg shell at a muzzle velocity of 670m/sec with a maximum penetration of 91mm of armour (British standard of 50 per cent chance of perforation, homogeneous armour, angled at 30 degrees), which did not permit the gun to penetrate the Hetzer's upper front armour. The lower front armour (60mm at 40 degrees) offered a line-of-sight thickness of 78mm, which could be penetrated at a range of about 500m. Photographic evidence from Lake Balaton also suggests that the Hetzer's gun mantlet and cast gun blister could be penetrated by 76mm shells due to its poor quality, although the range required for penetration is unknown. SU-76M crews were issued APCR shot to deal with heavy armour at ranges of 500m or less. This shot could penetrate up to 128mm of armour (Soviet standard of 80 per cent chance of perforation, homogeneous armour, 90 degrees) at 100m, meaning that at point-blank range, the SU-76M still had a chance. The Hetzer's thin side and rear armour could be penetrated at effectively any range even by the ZIS-3's HE shell.

The ZIS-3 gun shared ammunition with field-artillery guns, and thus had access to a large number of other rounds. These included the 6.2kg 53-O-350-A HE shell with 710g of HE filler, or shrapnel and canister shot for anti-infantry combat. The Jagdpanzer 38 only had access to one shell for use against 'soft' targets: the 5.74kg 7.5cm Sprenggranate 34 with 660g of HE filler. With a smaller explosive filler and lower overall mass, HE shells fired by the Jagdpanzer 38 created fewer lethal fragments and dispersed them over a smaller area.

CREW

The driver of the SU-76M sat alone in the driver's compartment in the front of the vehicle. He was flanked by the engine and transmission compartment to his right and the fuel tanks to his left. His hatch door could be opened while driving for better visibility, but he could only look through a rotating MK-4 periscope when it was closed. He could communicate with the commander by means of a TPU-3F intercom or a system of indicator lights.

Members of the gun crew, consisting of the commander, gunner and loader, were located in the fighting compartment in the rear. The commander sat to the right of the gun. He observed the battlefield through a MK-4 periscope and also had a separate TR-4 periscope for fire correction. He could use a direct-vision slit, protected by bulletproof glass and an armoured shutter, to observe the terrain directly in front of his vehicle. In addition to commanding the vehicle, he operated a 12RT-3 or 9RS radio installed in the fighting compartment to his right.

In battle, the gunner stood to the left of the gun or sat on a folding seat. He used a PG-1M Goerz-type panoramic sight with a 4× magnification and 10.5-degree field of view to aim the gun and a foot pedal to fire. He also had a MK-4 periscope for observation of the battlefield.

The loader stood in the back of the fighting compartment or sat on a folding seat on the rear plate, behind the gunner. He had no vision devices of his own,

BELOW LEFT
Fighting compartment of the SU-76M, gunner's station. A DT-29 machine gun is shown installed in the pistol port to the gunner's left. This weapon was used for close defence and was not usually mounted here. (Author)

BELOW RIGHT
Fighting compartment of the SU-76M, commander's station. This photo shows a wealth of observation devices available to the commander as well as a signal panel for communication with the driver and a radio set. A PPSh-41 submachine gun is mounted to his right on the side of the fighting compartment. (Author)

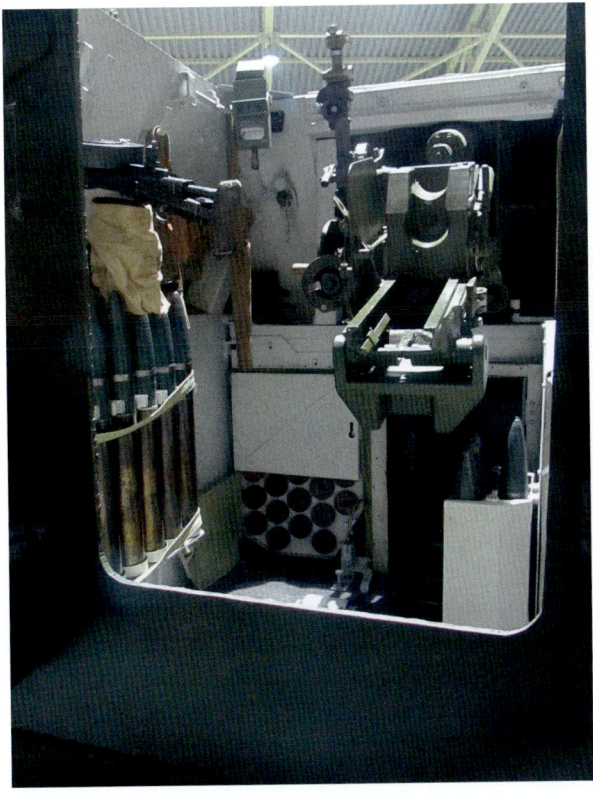

but could use the pistol ports on the left and right of the fighting compartment. His workspace was relatively open and spacious, allowing for a maximum rate of fire of 20rd/min for the gun.

The crew of the Jagdpanzer 38 consisted of four crewmen: the driver, gunner, loader and commander. The driver sat in the front of the vehicle (there was no separation between the fighting and driver's compartments). He observed through a vision slit protected by armoured glass in the front of the hull or two fixed periscopes, depending on the version of the vehicle. The gunner sat behind the driver, observing through a 5× Sfl ZF1a gunsight offering a field of view of 8 degrees.

The loader sat at the back of the fighting compartment. In addition to loading the gun, he serviced the machine gun. He could observe through either the machine-gun sight or a periscope fixed in the 9 o'clock position. The driver, gunner and loader all entered the vehicle through the hatch above the loader's station.

The commander sat on the right side of the fighting compartment. He entered the vehicle through his own hatch, which was also used to mount a binocular periscope for observation. With the hatches closed, his only means of vision was a fixed periscope facing backwards. He also operated the Fu 5 radio set. Because the set was mounted on the rear left of the fighting compartment, behind the loader, this could not be done without the loader's assistance, however. The radio antenna was installed on the right side of the hull. On a commander's vehicle, an Fu 8 radio set was provided on the left side of the hull and an additional antenna was installed on the left side.

BELOW LEFT
The loader's station in the Hetzer. Since the commander could not reach the radio, the loader was the vehicle's de facto radio operator. (Author)

BELOW RIGHT
The commander's station in the Deutsches Panzermuseum Munster's Hetzer. Located between the protruding engine compartment bulkhead and side of the hull, the commander had very little space to move around. His single rear-facing periscope can be seen in this photo. It would be difficult to turn around in order to use it in this confined space with the hatches closed. (Author)

While the Jagdpanzer 38 surpassed the SU-76M when it came to armour protection and armament, it fell far behind in crew comfort. The requirement to make a light vehicle with thick armour resulted in a very cramped workspace. The fighting compartment was just 135cm tall, meaning that it was impossible for any of the crewmen to stand. With such a low ceiling, it was also impossible to climb over the gun's recoil guard and move from the commander's half of the hull to the other half with the hatches closed.

While in most tanks the loader has one half of the turret in which to work due to the amount of space required to handle long rounds of ammunition, in the Jagdpanzer 38 he was squeezed into the same space as the gunner and driver. The gun was moved as far to the right as possible to free up space for him, but all that achieved was cramping the commander, who did not have enough space in his side of the fighting compartment to fit his equipment and as a result had to reach over to the other side of the vehicle to operate the radio. The commander also got in the way of half of the ammunition stored in the Jagdpanzer 38. His cramped workspace made it difficult for him to reach rounds and hand them to the loader or to get out of the way so that the loader could reach the rounds himself.

The narrow and low fighting compartment also made it difficult for the driver to enter his station, as he had to pull himself over both his own seat and the gunner's seat with a restricted range of movement. When using the controls, movement in the driver's station was also very restrictive. The gunner would follow the driver in, pressing his knees up against the removable backrest of the driver's seat. The gunner himself sat on a simple perch. There was no room for a backrest, as the loader needed as much space as possible in order to work in such a confined space. Only a few rounds would be available to the loader at a time without the assistance of other crewmen.

ABOVE LEFT

This view from above shows the Hetzer commander's seat (top left), loader's seat (top right) and gunner's seat (right). The amount of space inside the vehicle is very limited, making it difficult to move around inside a stationary Hetzer even without other crewmen present. (Author)

ABOVE RIGHT

The driver sat at the front of the Hetzer. To get to his station, he had to climb over the loader's and gunner's seats and then install a removable backrest to have any semblance of comfort. (Author)

Having had the opportunity to examine the Jagdpanzer 38s on display at the Deutsches Panzermuseum Munster and Canadian Tank Museum, the author can confirm that even without any other crewmen in the vehicle and the hatches open, moving around a stationary Jagdpanzer 38 was very difficult.

The rate of fire of the Jagdpanzer 38's gun is often given as 10-15rd/min, but that figure is only correct for the Jagdpanzer IV, which mounted the same gun in a much larger fighting compartment. It would be impossible for the cramped Jagdpanzer 38 to achieve the same rate of fire. Meanwhile, the SU-76M with its half-open fighting compartment could achieve a peak rate of fire of 20rd/min. The SU-76M's rate of fire was not constrained by the concentration of fumes, whereas the Jagdpanzer 38's crew relied on the vehicle's engine to draw fumes out of the fighting compartment.

The difference in available vision was also a stark one. The only crewmen whose sighting implements were comparable were the two loaders, both of whom could look to the left: the Jagdpanzer 38's loader using the fixed periscope and the SU-76M's using a pistol port.

Both drivers had access to an observation device pointing forward, but while the SU-76M's driver could open the hatch to see better outside of combat, the Jagdpanzer 38's driver could not. The SU-76M's periscope could also rotate and tilt, while the vision device of the Jagdpanzer 38 driver was fixed.

Both gunners looked through similar sights (the Jagdpanzer 38 had a slightly higher magnification, but a slightly narrower field of view). The SU-76M's gunner also had access to a MK-4 rotating periscope to spot his targets, but the Jagdpanzer 38's gunner could only be guided to a target by the commander.

The vision available to the commanders of the two vehicles was also very different. The commander of the SU-76M had access to two MK-4 periscopes (one facing forward and one to the right), a TR-4 periscope for fire correction and a direct-vision slit in the frontal armour. He also had unmagnified vision to the right by means of a pistol port and his view backwards was unimpeded. Meanwhile, the commander of the Jagdpanzer 38 was almost completely blind when his hatches were closed, having only the ability to see backwards through his fixed rear-facing periscope. He could only spot targets ahead of the vehicle by opening the hatch and extending a binocular periscope, in which case the hatch could no longer be used to enter or exit the vehicle.

As a result of these restrictions, the SU-76M by comparison had very good visibility. Two crewmen had 360-degree vision through rotating periscopes and if necessary, could look forward or to the sides through fixed ports. Vision to the rear was also unimpeded due to the casemate being open to the rear. Meanwhile, the Jagdpanzer 38's crew had almost no ability to look to the right and each crewman could only look in one direction (with the exception of the commander, who could look forward by opening his hatch and mounting the binocular periscope). In these conditions, the crew of the SU-76M enjoyed a clear view of the battlefield and could react to changing conditions, while the crew of the Jagdpanzer 38 could only fight a target directly in front of them, with only a limited ability to react to a threat appearing to one side or the other.

MOBILITY

The SU-76M was powered by a GAZ-203 power plant, consisting of two GAZ-70 petrol engines, producing a total of 140PS. Two fuel tanks holding a total of 412 litres of petrol gave the vehicle a cruising range of up to 320km. Top speed was 43km/h, but it was governed to 30km/h. At a mass of only 10.6 tonnes, giving a power-to-weight ratio of 13.3PS/tonne, the vehicle was quite agile, with an average speed of 34.1km/h on the highway (if a governor was not used) and 21.5km/h off-road. A gearbox from the ZIS-5 truck was used, giving four speeds forward and one reverse.

Each of the SU-76M's tracks was composed of 72 identical metallic track links, 300mm wide. Six road wheels with rubber tyres and three all-metal return rollers guided the track. Each road wheel had its own suspension arm and torsion bar. The idler in the rear was identical to the road wheels and its position could be adjusted to control track tension. The running gear and suspension elements were common with the T-70B light tank.

The SU-76M took its running gear and many automotive components from existing Soviet vehicles. This made it cheaper and faster to put into production. (Author)

The Hetzer's running gear, showing a bogie with a leaf spring and the single return roller hidden by sheet-metal dust shields. The running gear was based on that of the PzKpfw 38(t) nA reconnaissance tank originally pitched in 1942. (Author)

The Jagdpanzer 38 was powered by the Praga AE petrol engine. Two fuel tanks (220 litres on the right and 100 litres on the left) gave the vehicle a cruising range of 185km. A Praga-Wilson gearbox offered five speeds forward and one reverse. Top speed in fifth gear was 42km/h but with a mass of 16 tonnes giving a power-to-weight ratio of 10.2PS/tonne, the Jagdpanzer 38 had trouble making that speed, averaging 25km/h on the highway and 15km/h off-road. The engine was also the primary method of ventilation, air being drawn from the fighting compartment through a rectangular cowling. Cooling could be controlled by means of a sliding shutter.

The Jagdpanzer 38's running gear was identical to that used on the PzKpfw 38(t) nA reconnaissance tank, with the exception of thicker leaf springs to make up for the greater weight. There were four road wheels per side, collected into two bogies of two, each one of which had its own leaf spring. Only one return roller was installed per side. Both the return rollers and road wheels had rubber tyres. Each track had 96–98 identical metallic track links, 293mm-wide. The idler was located in the rear, combined with a track-tensioning mechanism. Five different types of idlers could be installed, with different numbers of circular openings to lighten the weight of the running gear.

The two vehicles had comparable engines, but with the Jagdpanzer 38 being half again as heavy, it had a much poorer power-to-weight ratio, which resulted in a poorer average speed than the SU-76M in any conditions. Likewise, the lighter SU-76M had superior ground pressure (0.57kg/cm² compared to the Jagdpanzer 38's 0.85kg/cm²) and therefore better mobility on soft soil. It was not for nothing that the *Nachrichtenblatt der Panzertruppen* (Newsletter for the Armoured Forces) for October 1944 warned

A knocked-out Jagdpanzer 38 in Prague, May 1945. Track extensions are installed. This was one way to improve the vehicle's poor ground pressure caused by the Hetzer's narrow tracks, but these attachments were fragile and bent or broke off easily when they hit obstacles. (Azoor Photo/Alamy Stock Photo)

against deploying the Jagdpanzer 38 alongside fully mechanized units as it would be too slow to keep up and suffer mechanical breakdowns when forced to move quickly. A warning against fighting in poor terrain was also made.

While the Jagdpanzer 38 had good armament and armour for its size and weight, Aleksey Surin had to make sacrifices in every other aspect of the design. The vehicle was cramped, blind and underpowered. Its opponent, while lacking the armour and armament of a dedicated tank destroyer, was much faster, more agile and could stay in the fight longer due to its superior fuel and ammunition capacity.

A North Korean SU-76M with a US M26 heavy tank, Korea, December 1950. North Korea received 176 SU-76Ms in total. (Corporal Wolfe/Wikimedia/Public Domain)

THE COMBATANTS

THE SOVIET SPG REGIMENT

The Red Army's first SPG regiments began forming in December 1942 based on TO&E #08/158. The regiment was composed of two batteries of SU-122 medium SPGs and four batteries of SU-76 light SPGs. Each battery consisted of two platoons of two vehicles each. In addition, the regiment contained an HQ platoon with the commander's SU-76, an ammunition supply platoon, a quartermaster platoon, a motorized transport platoon, a medical section and an artillery workshop. The regiment numbered 307 men, 17 SU-76s and eight SU-122s. These regiments entered the Reserve of the Supreme Command and were temporarily allocated to tank and mechanized units to reinforce them during critical operations.

The authorized strength was quickly revised. Regiments forming in 1943 followed TO&E #08/191 with an authorized strength of 289 men, eight SU-76s and 12 SU-122s. As before, vehicles were split into batteries of two platoons of two vehicles each. The total number of batteries was reduced to five (two SU-76 and three SU-122). There was no longer an SPG in the HQ platoon.

The mixed-regiment structure did not last long either. TO&E #010/456 was introduced in April 1943, authorizing a new regiment composed entirely of SU-76s. There were now 21 SU-76s per regiment, with five batteries of four vehicles each and one vehicle for the regiment commander. The supporting elements remained the same, however, for a total of 253 men per regiment. In October 1943 this structure changed slightly: TO&E #010/484 defined a 225-man regiment with four batteries of five vehicles each, plus one in the HQ. Batteries were no longer divided into platoons. Although at this point the SU-76M had entirely supplanted the SU-76 in

An SU-76M in Berlin, 1945. The vehicle carries a small branch, no doubt a remnant of a much more elaborate attempt at camouflaging the vehicle. Twisted remains of the right mudguard can be seen, suggesting that the vehicle's journey up to this point was not easy. (Imwar/Alamy Stock Photo)

production, no distinction is made by the TO&E or most other Red Army documents. By the end of 1943, sufficient numbers of SU-76s were available to begin replacing towed tank-destroyer artillery regiments in tank and mechanized corps with SU-76 regiments. Starting in mid-1943, a regiment of light SPGs was also attached to cavalry corps.

The success of the SU-76 in 1944 led to the introduction of light SPG brigades in January 1944 (TO&E #010/508). Each brigade consisted of an HQ company (two T-70 tanks and three M3A1 scout cars), three light SPG battalions, a motorized infantry battalion, an anti-aircraft company, a maintenance company and a medical platoon. Each battalion consisted of an HQ platoon with one T-70, four batteries of five SU-76s each, a supply platoon, a medical section and a quartermaster section. In total, the light SPG brigade numbered 1,122 men, 60 SU-76s, five T-70s and three M3A1 scout cars. Each tank army was now allocated one light SPG brigade instead of two light SPG regiments.

TO&E #04/434, approved in early 1944, defined a new type of SPG battalion. This battalion was permanently attached to an infantry division and was somewhat smaller than the battalions in light SPG brigades. It consisted of 12 SU-76s in three batteries of four vehicles each and numbered 184 men. Later in 1944 these battalions were enlarged to five vehicles per battery and one additional SU-76 for the commander, for a total of 16 SU-76s and 152 men.

Small numbers of SU-76s could also be included in other SPG brigades. Medium SPG brigades formed in December 1944 according to TO&E #010/500 contained a reconnaissance company equipped with three SU-76s.

As of 9 May 1945, the Red Army included seven light SPG brigades, 119 light SPG regiments and 70 battalions attached to infantry divisions. As of 5 March 1945, the 3rd Ukrainian Front at Lake Balaton had several SPG units in its composite formations.

Four light SPG regiments (the 1896th, 1891st, 1202nd and 864th) were subordinated directly to the 3rd Ukrainian Front.

There were also light SPG battalions: the 122nd as well as the 8th, 13th, 75th, 88th and 44th Guards in the 4th Guards Army. Despite an impressive number of units, the 4th Guards Army was heavily depleted and only had 26 SU-76s in total. The aforementioned 1891st Light SPG Regiment, also attached to the 4th Guards Army, had just two SU-76s.

Other Soviet armies of the 3rd Ukrainian Front had even fewer SPGs. The 72nd Light SPG Battalion in the 26th Army was also down to just two SU-76s and the 1202nd SPG Regiment assigned to reinforce it had 14. The 27th Army had the fewest number of SU-76s of all, with only seven in the 432nd Light SPG Battalion. The 57th Army, the furthest away from where the main fighting was going to take place, had a fair number of SU-76s: 21 in the 864th SPG Regiment allocated by the Front, held in the army commander's reserve.

Non-infantry formations also had SU-76s. The 18th Tank Corps had 12 on strength within the 1438th SPG Regiment, and the 208th SPG Brigade attached to the 18th Tank Corps had three more within the 1016th SPG Regiment. The 3rd Ukrainian Front's 1896th SPG Regiment with eight SU-76s was attached to the 5th Guards Cavalry Corps. Both corps were positioned in the centre of the 26th Army's defences: the 18th Tank Corps on the western side of the Sárvíz, the 5th Guards Cavalry Corps on the eastern side.

The introduction of the SU-76 into service coincided with reforms within the Red Army's armoured forces. On 7 December 1942 the GABTU (Main Automobile and Armour Directorate) was split up into the GBTU (Main Armour Directorate) and GAVTU (Main Automobile Directorate). The newly formed GBTU contained the USA (Self-Propelled Artillery Directorate) staffed by personnel transferred from the GAU (Main Artillery Directorate). Although the GAU still had influence over the development and use of SPGs, tanks and SPGs were now largely managed under one roof. This included the Self-Propelled Gun Training Centre and its three SPG training regiments as well as the two schools specializing in the training of SPG officers: the 2nd Kiev and 2nd Rostov schools. A third SPG school was formed in Kotlas, Arkhangelsk Oblast, on 17 March 1944.

This reorganization also coincided with a change in approach to training. The period of eight months for tank and SPG crewmen was no longer considered sufficient and was increased to one year starting in 1943. Additionally, efforts were made to pick out experienced enlisted men and NCOs for retraining into the armoured forces. A cadet with no prior military experience would have been a rare sight.

Cadets would go through thorough training, much of which overlapped with training in a regular artillery unit. Cadets learned to scout the area to pick out, prepare and camouflage positions for their SPGs, fight individually or as a battery, on the defensive or when accompanying infantry as a part of an attack. Much attention was paid to the operation of the SPG: maintenance and storage of the weapon and its ammunition; inspection before and after battle; and of course gunnery in various conditions, against stationary and moving targets, over open sights and indirectly, by using gunnery tables. Unlike artillerymen, future SPG crewmen also had to study the chassis of their gun, including driving, maintenance, operation of the radio and

An SU-76M in the streets of Budapest, 1956. The mudguards are flipped up, normally done to make track and idler maintenance easier. A tarpaulin covers the roof of the vehicle to protect its interior from rain. The pistol port is open, its cover hanging on by a chain, perhaps to allow the gunner to see while his usual vision devices are covered up. (Metzger, Jack, ETH-Bibliothek Zürich/Wikimedia/CC BY-SA 4.0)

relevant military engineering (including preparation of bridges and demolition of obstacles). Driver training included 80 hours of driving wheeled vehicles, 70 hours of driving auxiliary tracked vehicles and 120 hours of driving the SU-76 itself. Like any other soldiers, the training programme for SPG crewmen included marching drill, physical fitness (hand-to-hand combat, skiing, swimming, gymnastics), navigation and orienteering, as well as defence against chemical attack. A report card containing a record of this training was issued to each graduate and would be presented to the officers in the unit in which they arrived after graduation.

Once a newly minted SPG crewman reached his destination unit, his training was far from over. Newly established units underwent cohesion exercises in order to get used to fighting as a group. This gave the opportunity for vehicle and unit commanders to get used to each other's quirks as well. Training typically continued once the SPG unit left its base and was attached to a larger formation. Field commanders were often unsatisfied with the training received by new arrivals, however, in part because they were able to receive and process combat experience much faster than the SPG academy. As a result of this, freshly incoming personnel could receive additional training deemed necessary by their new superiors. Depending on the time permitted by the situation, this additional training could involve a full course lasting dozens of hours.

Training in anticipation of specific conditions was also conducted. When the seasons changed, all crews would receive refresher training on operating their vehicles in winter snow, spring mud or summer heat. Because it was known that the enemy was gathering a large tank force, all armoured units of the 3rd Ukrainian Front conducted additional anti-tank training in anticipation of the coming enemy offensive.

THE GERMAN TANK-DESTROYER BATTALION

Jagdpanzer 38 'Hetzer' tank destroyers were deployed as a part of tank-destroyer battalions subordinate to an army (*Armee Panzerjäger-Abteilungen*) or to the high command (*Heeres Panzerjäger-Abteilungen*). These battalions contained three companies of 14 vehicles each with three more in the HQ platoon for a total of 45 vehicles per battalion. Brand-new Hetzer units were not formed. Rather, existing units that already had experience with towed or self-propelled anti-tank guns were rearmed with these tank destroyers. For example, Heeres Panzerjäger-Abteilung 731 was formed in November 1943 from elements of existing tank-destroyer battalions. The HQ came from Panzerjäger-Abteilung 225 and the composite companies were taken from Panzerjäger-Abteilungen 188, 175 and 255. Heeres Panzerjäger-Abteilung 731 was then issued 45 Hetzers and four Bergepanzer 38 ARVs on the same chassis in July 1944.

Hetzers were also issued to individual companies within tank-destroyer battalions within *Heer* and Waffen-SS divisions. Like companies in Hetzer battalions, these nominally contained 14 vehicles each. However, the poor situation with *matériel* by 1945 could mean that the number of functional vehicles was much lower. Additionally, Hetzers could be replaced with captured vehicles or even towed guns.

A number of these companies and battalions gathered at Lake Balaton by 5 March 1945, of which the 71. Infanterie-Division had seven functional Hetzers in its Panzerjäger-Abteilung 171.

The history of Panzerjäger-Abteilung 171 dates back to the formation of the 71. Infanterie-Division in the reserves of Wehrkreis XI (11th Military District). Owing to the resolute will and unparalleled skill required to stand strong in the face of a tank assault, only the best recruits were chosen for tank-destroyer battalions. After 12–16 weeks of basic training, recruits trained with the 3.7cm anti-tank gun in addition to regular field infantry tactics. To augment drill and training, Panzerjäger-Abteilung 171 had the experience of the campaign in France under its belt and was no stranger to facing heavily armoured enemy tanks.

Periscopes available to the Hetzer's driver as shown on the vehicle at the Deutsches Panzermuseum Munster. One periscope was tilted forward to provide near vision, the other upright for looking into the distance. (Author).

This battalion was completely destroyed at Stalingrad with the rest of its division and was re-formed from scratch beginning in March 1943 in Jutland. The elite training standards that made the German tank-destroyer branch a foe to be reckoned with were relaxed after the defeat at Stalingrad in order to bring units to combat readiness more quickly. More powerful 75mm PaK 40 guns, which were now available in sufficient numbers to replace the old 3.7cm and 5cm PaK 38, had to make up the gap in training.

Once re-formed, the 71. Infanterie-Division was sent to Italy to disarm Italian troops, but was bogged down in heavy fighting around Cassino. The heavily depleted division was withdrawn in July 1944 and reconstituted again. After a retreat from the Gothic Line under heavy pressure from British Commonwealth forces, the division had to be pulled out of the fighting once again. The division and its composite units were recalled to Trieste for refitting and refresher training in September 1944. This was also where Panzerjäger-Abteilung 171 replaced its outdated Marder III tank destroyers and confiscated Italian SPGs with more modern Hetzers.

Despite receiving a new kind of vehicle with much stronger armour, the tactics of the *Panzerjäger* remained the same. German tank destroyers fought in much the same way as their towed anti-tank guns, from prepared defensive positions. As before, the greatest protection was not considered to be the Hetzer's frontal armour, but the ability to engage the enemy at long range and withdraw before coming under return fire.

The battalion relocated to Hungary in mid-October and was attached to the LXVIII. Armeekorps in the 2. Panzerarmee, the formation within which it witnessed the opening of Operation *Spring Awakening*.

ABOVE LEFT
The Hetzer's gunsight, as viewed from the outside. This was the gunner's only means of observing the battlefield. (Author)

ABOVE RIGHT
Hetzer at the Canadian Tank Museum showing both vision devices available to the commander: a binocular periscope facing forwards and a fixed periscope facing backwards. With the hatches closed, the commander was almost completely blind. (Author)

THE HUNGARIAN ASSAULT ARTILLERY BATTALION

The unit with the most Hetzers to be deployed at Lake Balaton was Hungarian. Hetzers in Hungarian Army service were deployed as a part of assault artillery battalions (*rohamtüzér osztályok*).

Hungary began to prepare for the organization of an assault artillery force in 1942. With the Hungarian Army lacking any experience in this area, a commission was established to examine German methods. Hungarian officers went through German artillery training and returned home to set up what would come to be known as Royal Hungarian Assault Artillery. Training of the first of the new artillerymen according to German methods began on 1 March 1943. An inspection in the summer of 1943 by Chief of the General Staff Colonel-General (*Vezérezredes*) Ferenc Szombathelyi confirmed that the assault artillery branch was a promising one, and authorization was given for the creation of seven new assault artillery battalions. The existing personnel training at Hajmáskér were reorganized into the 1st Assault Artillery Battalion, a training unit that was to provide personnel for the other six battalions. Colonel (*Ezredes*) Ernő Billnitzer, a field artillery officer, was placed in charge of the newly formed force.

Owing to the need to have Hungarian assault artillery battalions battle-ready by the spring of 1944, Billnitzer decided to retrain field-artillery personnel. The battalions were intended to be elite units and there was no shortage of volunteers, with three applicants for every available spot. In addition to operating the assault guns themselves, newly minted assault gunners studied tactics and organization, signals, first aid and physical fitness. Training was organized by 5 August 1943. In addition to the skills learned by the 1st Assault Artillery Battalion, the incoming assault artillery troops learned how to ride motorcycles, drive trucks and cars and to repair and maintain their equipment. A second training course was organized for officers. Courses for NCOs and drivers ran in parallel. Radio operators, drivers and gunners received special training as a part of a separate course. In anticipation of delivery of German vehicles to Hungarian assault artillery battalions, 16 officers, 24 drivers and eight mechanics went through an advanced German course at the Assault Gun School (*Sturmgeschützschule*) Burg, north-east of Magdeburg.

New assault artillery battalions also began forming at this time. Training was meant to include cohesion exercises with each battalion's designated infantry division, but due to the rapidly approaching front line this was not completed. Organization of the new battalions was completed on 1 April 1944 and training ended on 14 April. As the situation on the front lines deteriorated, the battalions were included in the order of battle on 17 May. Their readiness was assessed in large-scale combined-arms exercises held on 26 May, which proved that Hungary's newest type of armoured unit was ready for action.

The initially planned organization of an assault artillery battalion consisted of a staff company (one assault gun) that also contained a motorized pioneer platoon, a signals platoon, a motorcycle platoon, a service section and a medical platoon.

Zrínyi II assault gun knocked out in Budapest, spring 1945. Originally, the Hungarian assault artillery battalions were supposed to be armed with these assault guns, but due to shortages they could have Hetzers, StuGs or even towed guns. (History and Art Collection/Alamy Stock Photo)

The remainder of a battalion's assault guns would be split between three batteries of ten guns each. In turn, each battery consisted of the commander's assault gun, three platoons of three assault guns each, a medical section and a repair section. A workshop company for short- and medium-term repair as well as a transport company equipped with heavy tractors were included for maintenance. In reality, only 70 per cent of the officers and 50 per cent of the enlisted men originally planned could be provided, although the number of vehicles still officially stood at 31 assault guns. Owing to shortages of vehicles, however, not all of the battalions received their full complement of assault guns. Men without a vehicle fought as mechanized infantry.

The assault artillery battalions were supposed to be armed with the 105mm Zrínyi II assault gun and each unit was issued three vehicles built from mild steel for training. Damage to the Manfréd Weiss factory in Budapest by Allied bombers, however, led to Zrínyi II production ending prematurely. Insufficient numbers of the Zrínyi II meant that only a few of the new assault artillery battalions – the 1st, 10th and one battery of the 20th – were armed with Hungarian vehicles. The 7th Assault Artillery Battalion was equipped with StuGs, but the rest of the units were issued Hetzers or Turán medium tanks instead.

Hungary began receiving Hetzers starting in August 1944, ten of which were attached to the 1st Cavalry Division (*Lovashadosztály*), which fought at Warsaw as a part of the IV. SS-Panzerkorps. A battery of Hetzers fought as a part of the Billnitzer Assault Artillery Group personally commanded by Billnitzer in Budapest. Various sources state that this battery belonged to the 20th, 24th or 25th Assault Artillery Battalion. Regardless, the battery was lost when Budapest fell to Soviet forces in February 1945.

Three additional shipments of 25 Hetzers each were made to the Hungarian Army in December 1944 and January 1945. Some were issued to the 20th Assault Artillery Battalion (tactical numbers T-01 to T-040) and 25th Assault Artillery Battalion (tactical numbers K-041 to K-075). Hungarian Army tactical numbers were painted directly over German markings and camouflage, still bearing German *Balkenkreuz* insignia.

Of particular interest to the subject matter of this book is the 20th Assault Artillery Battalion. This unit was based in Eger and commanded by Captain (*Százados*) József Henkey-Hőnig, with First Lieutenant (*Főhadnagy*) Imre Kömlődy assigned as the AFV instructor. Henkey-Hőnig was an experienced officer and also the leader of the second

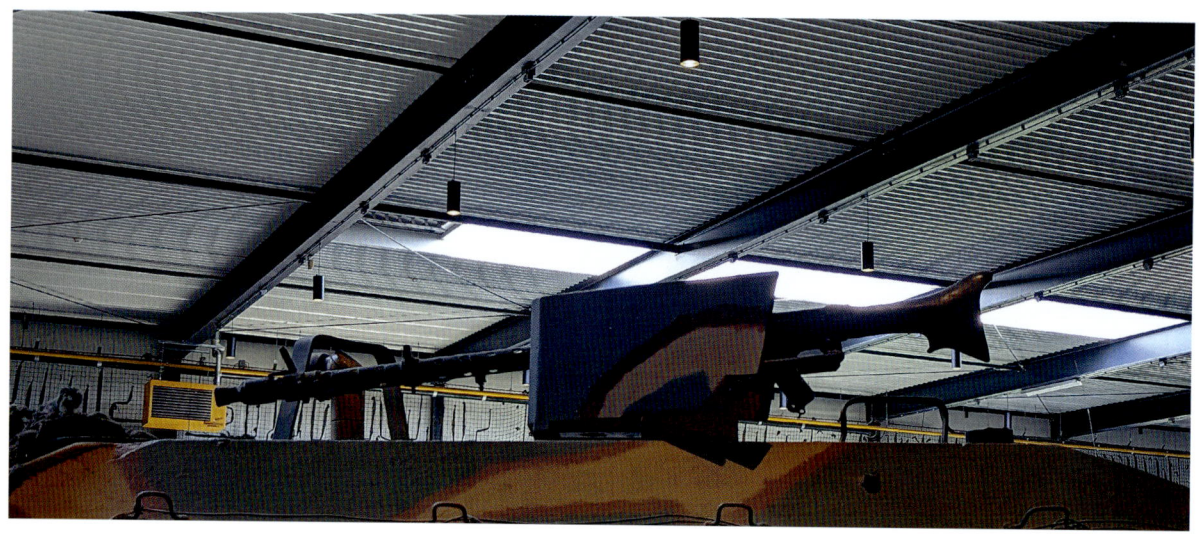

An MG 34 machine gun mounted on the roof of the Hetzer at Oorlogsmuseum Overloon. This machine gun could be fired either from inside the vehicle or by a crewman taking cover behind the gun shield. (Author)

officer-training course, established at Hajmáskér. As mentioned above, the 20th Assault Artillery Battalion was one of three to receive a battery of Hungarian Zrínyi II self-propelled howitzers. The other two batteries had to make do with 15 Hetzers between them.

The 20th Assault Artillery Battalion was attached to the elite Szent-László Division raised in October 1944. The division, named after Hungary's most revered saint, was built around three of General Major (*Vezérőrnagy*) Zoltán Szügyi's paratrooper regiments. Szügyi chose the supporting units himself, aiming for those that had distinguished themselves in action. The Szent-László Division first saw battle on 19 December 1944, fighting north of Budapest at the Garam and Ipoly rivers to secure the retreat of German and Hungarian forces. This fighting took a heavy toll but nevertheless, the 20th Assault Artillery Battalion – still under the command of Henkey-Hőnig, now a major (*Őrnagy*) – was ready to take part in Operation *Spring Awakening*.

At the time, the 20th Assault Artillery Battalion was assigned to the 25th Infantry Division. The battalion had a chance to test its new Hetzers in combat before *Spring Awakening* during a limited attack carried out at Lepsény, north-east of Lake Balaton, on 16 and 26 February 1945. Despite drawing heavily from German assault-gun doctrine, the Hungarians practised their own tactics. These early battles resulted in the first victories for Hungarian Hetzers, but also revealed a critical weakness: the narrow tracks sank in mud to the point where two other Hetzers could not recover one that was stuck. This was an important lesson for the main battle that was yet to come.

The 20th Assault Artillery Battalion was subordinate to the 6. SS-Panzerarmee, putting it in the midst of the action between lakes Balaton and Velence. By March 1945, the battalion was a battle-hardened formation put together from experienced officers and enlisted men. As of 5 March 1945, the battalion had a total of 36 Hetzers available, 22 of which were in fighting order.

Both the German and Hungarian tank-destroyer units received their Hetzers only a few months before Operation *Spring Awakening*. All units were battle-hardened, however, and consisted of experienced anti-tank gunners who were able to put an anti-tank gun to good use, regardless of what chassis it was mounted on.

COMBAT

THE MAIN AXIS

Operation *Spring Awakening* began on 6 March 1945 with three simultaneous thrusts. In the south, the XCI. Armeekorps crossed the Drava River at 0100hrs and engaged the 1st Bulgarian Army. At 0600hrs, the 2. Panzerarmee struck in the west against the Soviet 57th Army. Finally, the main offensive began at 0847hrs. Following a half-hour-long artillery barrage, the 6. SS-Panzerarmee and Armeegruppe Balck moved into the gap between lakes Balaton and Velence. In particular, the I. Kavalleriekorps with supporting Hungarian Army units attacked southwards from the eastern bank of Lake Balaton, aiming towards Enying.

The Axis assault was not as decisive as it could have been. Low cloud cover impeded German air support and the spring thaw, which reached +11 degrees Celsius, turned the ground into mud. The armada of armoured vehicles that the Germans gathered for this offensive was paralyzed. Despite the volume and duration of German artillery fire, it was generally ineffective and failed to incapacitate Soviet gun batteries. In return, the Soviet batteries also opened fire on concentrations of German troops that were revealed by reconnaissance.

Nevertheless, the Germans knew where to attack. As the II. SS-Panzerkorps and III. Panzerkorps struck between the 4th Guards Army and the 26th Army, the I. Kavalleriekorps, I. SS-Panzerkorps (which included the 1. *Leibstandarte SS Adolf Hitler* and 12. *Hitlerjugend* Panzer divisions) struck against the front of the 26th Army. The brunt of the attack came largely against the 68th Guards Rifle Division with some limited assistance from the neighbouring 233rd Rifle Division. Despite the relocation of two anti-tank artillery regiments to this sector, the defence could not hold. The Soviet units fell back behind the Sárvíz River to the next line of defence.

PREVIOUS PAGES
A Hetzer commander coordinating with supporting infantry. Despite being tank destroyers, Hetzers were often used to support infantry assaults during Operation *Spring Awakening* as their thick frontal armour made them effective when used as assault guns. Unfortunately, the weak engine and narrow tracks limited their mobility in muddy terrain and they were unable to support infantry away from roads.

To the west, the German offensive was not progressing as well. Elements of the 74th and 151st Rifle divisions defending to the south of Lake Balaton did not just hold against the German attack, but launched a counter-attack. The Germans noted that the cavalry corps managed to advance only 300m along the Siófok–Lepsény highway on 6 March. It was noted that the I. Kavalleriekorps came under constant counter-attacks from the direction of Enying. The ferocity of the fighting was underlined by an order given by Colonel-General Mitrofan I. Nedelin, Commander of Artillery of the 3rd Ukrainian Front, to transfer half of all available 76mm AP and APCR ammunition to the 26th Army. Despite this, both of the 26th Army's SU-76 units remained in reserve.

Despite having some effect in the main direction of attack, the progress of Operation *Spring Awakening* was unsatisfactory. General der Infanterie Otto Wöhler, the commander of Heeresgruppe Süd, reported to Guderian, by now Chief of the Army General Staff:

> Tanks can move across cross-country terrain with difficulty due to heavy mud, and all roads are turned into minefields and covered by enemy artillery. Infantry units could not achieve a rapid breakthrough and fierce fighting led to heavy expenditure of ammunition, as a result of which the soldiers may end up without bullets. It was discovered that the enemy was waiting for our offensive and prepared for it, even if the exact start time and direction of attack were unknown. (Quoted in Isayev & Kolomiets 2009: 133)

The weather was on the German side on 7 March. Even though thick fog limited visibility to 400m and prevented the use of air support, they could attack without fear of bombardment by Soviet artillery. Without the ability of Soviet anti-tank gun batteries to support one another, German armour began to grind down individual Soviet batteries and emplacements. As a result of repeated attacks on 7–8 March, the 68th Guards Rifle Division was forced to withdraw past Káloz. The 26th Army deployed its SPG regiments. The 1202nd SPG Regiment south of Káloz did not see battle on 7 March, but the 72nd Light SPG Battalion located on the western outskirts of Káloz made a stand, claiming the destruction of eight enemy tanks but losing both of its SU-76s. The regiment was withdrawn. Instead, the 22nd Tank Regiment (a mixed formation formed from a training regiment containing 11 T-34s, one KV-1S, one SU-85 and four SU-76s) arrived to take up positions in Dég, south of Káloz.

As the fighting intensified in the middle of the 26th Army's defences, the 18th Tank Corps was subordinated directly to the 26th Army in order to speed up coordination. The 1438th SPG Regiment was in turn attached to the 170th Tank Brigade. Three Axis attacks were beaten back that day for the loss of three SU-76s knocked out, six T-34s burned up and another two knocked out. The fighting on 9 March was tougher, with the Axis forces attacking by day and night. Nine attacks were repelled but Soviet losses were slight: two T-34s burned up and two more knocked out. Some territory was lost, with the Axis forces taking Hill 159 during a night-time attack. Over the next few days the 18th Tank Corps dug in at Sárosd, slowly pulling back under pressure from enemy attacks. The corps' SU-76 assets were taking a beating; it was down to nine fighting SU-76s on 9 March and two on 10 March. Only three SU-76s were written off, however, and nine more arrived on 11 March to reinforce the battered regiment. With repairs to

Even where anti-tank guns were absent, Red Army defences bristled with anti-tank rifles. Armour-piercing bullets were issued to riflemen and machine-gunners. Even if the bullets did not pierce the armour of enemy tanks, they could blind them by knocking out observation devices. This Hetzer shows two black stripes painted below the driver's observation port, designed to confuse enemy riflemen. (Author)

the surviving vehicles, it was possible to form five batteries, each of which supported a tank battalion. With its regained strength, the 1438th SPG Regiment stood strong against Axis attacks on 12–14 March until the order to counter-attack was given.

The other SU-76 regiment in the 18th Tank Corps, the 1016th SPG Regiment of the 208th SPG Brigade, took up defensive positions behind the gun belt formed by SU-100 tank destroyers near Csillag. This did not last long as the SU-76s were pressed into battle on 9 March, fighting in the first echelon in front of mechanized infantry as improvised tanks. They had some success in this role, being credited with the destruction of four enemy cannon during the morning attack. The SU-76 battery also claimed that they destroyed two Tiger tanks and knocked out one more when defending against a German attack that evening. While it is unlikely that these were actually Tigers, significant consumption of APCR shot suggests that even the light SPGs contributed to anti-tank defences. No SU-76s were lost that day. The 1016th SPG Regiment was not involved in any more fighting until 14 March, instead manoeuvring between reserve firing positions to remain ready to counter Axis breakthroughs.

The 1202nd SPG Regiment, now fighting to contain the enemy's progress east, lost one SU-76 at Seregélyes. Thanks to digging in on 8 March, the regiment was able to defend its positions successfully on 9 March with no losses. On that day the regiment was also reallocated from the 26th Army to the 27th Army. The latter's own 432nd SPG Battalion was still not engaged in any fighting; its personnel were undergoing training and preparing defensive positions at Perkáta, and its position did not change as of 11 March, even though the 27th Army began to take over positions from the battered 26th Army. This successful defence was not only due to the efforts of the Soviet guns and armour. Heeresgruppe Süd noted in its records that its armoured forces could not be deployed at Seregélyes to their full potential due to alternating periods of snow and mild weather turning the roads to mud.

SU-76M GUNSIGHT VIEW

An SU-76M gunner views a Hetzer through his PG-1M Goerz panoramic sight. With 60mm-thick highly sloped armour at the front offering a line-of-sight thickness of up to 120mm, the Hetzer presented a tough target to face head on. The armour-piercing shell fired by the SU-76M's 76mm ZIS-3 gun could only penetrate up to 104mm of armour at 100m. The only way to penetrate the Hetzer's front armour was to fire scarce tungsten carbide-core sub-calibre armour-piercing ammunition at very close range. On the other hand, the thin side armour, just 20mm thick and not as highly sloped, was vulnerable at effectively any distance from which the ZIS-3 could score a hit, even at an angle. The Hetzer's crew was hampered by a lack of vision devices and had very limited situational awareness, particularly to the right. If the SU-76M's crew spotted its opponent first, it would be very easy to sneak up from the side or rear unseen and deliver a killing blow.

HETZER GUNSIGHT VIEW

A Hetzer gunner guides his 7.5cm PaK 39 gun on target through his Sfl ZF1a gun sight offering 5× magnification. The PzGr 39 APCBC armour-piercing shell fired at a muzzle velocity of 750m/sec could penetrate up to 117mm of armour. The SU-76M was equipped with light bulletproof armour, up to 25mm at 60 degrees offering just 50mm line-of-sight thickness. This kind of light armour was enough to protect the SU-76M from shell splinters, as its intended role as a mechanized divisional gun would normally keep it out of direct fire. As one of the most common types of AFVs in the Red Army, however, it was often pressed into the role of an assault gun when no other armour was available, almost always resulting in heavy losses.

The 5th Guards Cavalry Corps remained in reserve on 8 March, but took part in repelling German attacks on 9 March. The corps' SU-76s were split into batteries and used to support cavalry battalions. Three SU-76s were kept in reserve by the commander of the 63rd Cavalry Division. The SU-76s distinguished themselves in this battle, holding back the enemy long enough for a key bridge to be demolished. The defence was conducted with no losses. Later that day the 1896th SPG Regiment was reallocated to the 11th Cavalry Division. On 10 March these SU-76s were used to destroy enemy beachheads across the Kapos Canal. German attacks grew increasingly fierce on 11–13 March, but an additional nine SU-76s arrived to replenish the cavalry's losses, making a total of 15. The newly reinforced 1896th SPG Regiment was attached to the 12th Cavalry Division and dug in to aid in the defence of the positions of the 41st and 43rd Cavalry regiments.

As early as two days into the German offensive, Soviet units were already being reallocated in preparation for a counter-attack. The 1891st SPG Regiment, battered during the January–February fighting, was removed from the 4th Guards Army on 8 March and reinforced to its authorized strength of 21 SPGs. The regiment did not take part in the fighting between lakes Balaton and Velence, but instead was reallocated into the reserves of the 57th Army. Newly arriving SU-76s were used to replenish other SPG regiments in the 3rd Ukrainian Front as well.

The Hungarians enjoyed some initial success. The 1st Battery of the 20th Assault Artillery Battalion supporting the 4. Kavallerie-Division entered Alsótekeres west of Enying, although they were thrown back by a Soviet counter-attack. German cavalry with support from Hungarian Hetzers also progressed east of Enying, where elements of the 3. Kavallerie-Division with support from the other two batteries of Hetzers was able to overcome a Soviet counter-attack and capture Attilapuszta farmstead. A force of 12 Hetzers along with the 20th Assault Artillery Battalion's anti-tank gun battery had to be called in again just a few hours later, after the German cavalry lost their positions. Despite losing the Hetzer used by the commander of the 3rd Battery to a mine, the Hungarian assault artillery was successful in this attack. Their luck turned quickly, however, when a Hetzer carrying a number of German officers hit a mine, resulting in the total loss of the vehicle and wounding some of the crew. The Germans chose to have their field briefing immediately on site, but a Soviet rocket artillery strike killed a number of German cavalry officers. The attack towards Hill 162 was not successful. A follow-up attack the next day took the hill and the farmstead upon it, but could not move further south due to Soviet minefields despite support from assault guns. The same attack was repeated on 8 March but the assault guns were once again bogged down by Soviet mines within minutes. The offensive only continued in the evening after engineers were called in to clear a passage through the mines.

The 20th Assault Artillery Battalion (with 15 operational Hetzers) and the 25th Infantry Division reached Enying with the I. Kavalleriekorps only on 10 March. Progress was still slow due to poor weather and the condition of the ground. Nevertheless, by 10 March the 4. Kavallerie-Division and the Hungarian Hetzers assaulted Enying while the 3. Kavallerie-Division seized a bridgehead over the Sió River. As a result of fighting during 9–11 March, Enying fell. The I. Kavalleriekorps and I. SS-Panzerkorps controlled the territory between the Sarviz Canal and the Sió, driving a deep wedge into the Soviet defences.

Hetzer tank destroyer at the Oorlogsmuseum Overloon. The wire wrapped around various hardpoints welded to the exterior armour was used to hold foliage, which broke up the vehicle's silhouette and made it harder to detect. (Author)

This breakthrough was also concerning for the 3rd Ukrainian Front. The 208th SPG Brigade was pulled out of its positions at Szőlőhegy–Seregélyes and sent to deal with the breakthrough on 11 March, leaving behind its 1016th SPG Regiment with the 18th Tank Corps. The 18th Tank Corps reported 13 SU-76s on strength as of 20 March.

The Hetzers of the 20th Assault Artillery Battalion continued along the shore of Lake Balaton. The 3. Kavallerie-Division was closing in on Balatonszabadi by 12 March and attacked Siófok on 13 March. Here, they were rebuffed, with six Hetzers reported as having been knocked out. Other sources state that this attack never took place due to losses and mechanical failure among the Hungarian Hetzers. Nevertheless, this was the extent of the progress of Axis forces along the shore of Lake Balaton. From this point on, the Germans had to dig in and fight against Soviet counter-attacks, protecting their beachheads across the Sió Canal.

The situation was not unique to this sector. Soviet reports noted that the German offensive had stopped gaining ground by 11 March. By 13 March, reports indicated that individual Axis units had stopped attacking and started to dig in to defend what little territory they had gained. A powerful Soviet artillery group gathered at Sárosd on the night of 11/12 March stopped the attack of the III. Panzerkorps and II. SS-Panzerkorps towards the Danube River. After a desperate last-ditch Axis effort on 15 March, attacks against the 27th Army ceased. Likewise, the I. SS-Panzerkorps reached the Kapos Canal on 11 March, but was unable fully to clear the Soviet presence on the northern shore or expand its beachheads on the southern shore. Attacks against the 26th Army in this sector ceased on the evening of 15 March.

By then it was clear that Operation *Spring Awakening* had failed. German–Hungarian positions were under constant attack by Soviet forces and could barely hold their ground. Poor weather and difficult terrain meant that supplies necessary to maintain a mechanized offensive could not be delivered. In the meantime, the Red Army was comfortable with the enemy's positions and prepared its own counter-offensive. The Germans noted a column of 3,000 vehicles gathering at Budapest. Their objective was clear: an attack in the south-west direction would cut off the Axis forces that poured into the gap between lakes Balaton and Velence. To stay put would be suicide. Not two weeks into their offensive that took months of preparation and the Panzerwaffe's last strength to carry out, the Germans began to pull back on the night of 15/16 March. The last German armoured offensive of World War II had penetrated only 30km west of the Sarviz Canal and 12km south of Lake Velence. The attack south of Lake Balaton was even less effective, with the 2. Panzerarmee advancing to a depth of just a few kilometres.

The retreat led to the reorganization of German forces. General der Panzertruppe Hermann Balck's 6. Armee was now responsible for the area between lakes Balaton and Velence, while SS-Oberstgruppenführer Josef Dietrich's 6. SS-Panzerarmee was moved north to cover the roads to Linz, Vienna and Munich, which were now open to the Red Army. As a part of this rotation, Balck assumed command of the I. Kavalleriekorps and its composite units as well as the 2nd Hungarian Army. Both commanders were scrambling for forces, and Dietrich argued for the return of the I. Kavalleriekorps, as horses were more suitable for fighting in thick forests than tanks. This request later proved fortuitous for the Hungarian units still attached to I. Kavalleriekorps.

On 21 March, the Hungarian 20th Assault Artillery Battalion was pulled out of the front line and sent for refitting. It reported 13 Hetzers on strength, but since the unit did not rejoin the fight, one can conclude that these vehicles were heavily damaged and could not be repaired.

Hungarian forces were hampered not just by the enemy, but by their own allies. Rumours that Hungarians were surrendering en masse reached German command. Reportedly, the 6. SS-Panzerarmee even encountered soldiers in Hungarian uniforms fighting alongside the Red Army. These rumours were fuelled by the fact that the Hungarians made for a convenient scapegoat to blame for the failure of the Panzerwaffe's last offensive. General der Infanterie Wöhler ordered that at the slightest hint of dissolution or intention to surrender, Hungarian units should be disarmed and used as labour troops for the Germans in platoon- and company-sized groups. The tense atmosphere is evidenced by the fact that all Hungarian units under Balck's command were disarmed and their motor vehicles confiscated. The aforementioned 20th Assault Artillery Battalion and 25th Infantry Division as well as the Szent-László Division under the 6. SS-Panzerarmee escaped this fate, however, fighting their way westward and surrendering to the British.

Typical ammunition as used by SU-76M SPGs: a high-explosive shell (top) and an armour-piercing shell (bottom). Their light weight and small size coupled with the open fighting compartment of the SU-76M allowed the ZIS-3 gun to reach a high rate of fire, on par with towed ZIS-3 field guns. (Author)

THE SOUTH-WESTERN AXIS

It was easy for the Germans to blame Hungarians for their failure, but the Germans themselves did not perform much better. The 2. Panzerarmee attacking south of Lake Balaton with the objective of capturing Kaposvár began its offensive at 0600hrs on 6 March, opposed by the Soviet 57th Army. Success at the end of the first day was limited. As in the north, the Germans started their offensive with a 45-minute artillery barrage, but here Soviet artillery opened fire in response, damaging attacking German forces and delaying the attack by 15 minutes.

The 57th Army reported repulsing 18 infantry attacks supported by small groups of armour. The total gain for the Germans that day was two farmsteads and the Jákó railway station. At 1000hrs on 6 March the 864th SPG Regiment was deployed from the 57th Army commander's reserve and attached to the 67th Rifle Corps to aid the 113th Rifle Division in retaking Jákó. The SPG units had spent two months conducting cohesion exercises with their riflemen and the two already knew how to work well together. The 2nd Battery attacked towards Balaskó in the north, while the 1st, 3rd and 4th batteries attacked Jákó directly. Here, they came face to face with Hetzers attached to Grenadier-Regimenter 194 and 211. Owing to the soft ground and ample minefields, however, the Hetzers did not make much of an impact. The grenadiers instead opted for *Panzerfaust* anti-tank launchers to combat Soviet armour. The II. Bataillon of Grenadier-Regiment 211 managed to take Szabotanya farmstead with the help of its Hetzers, but with heavy losses. German attacks stopped around midday. A Soviet counter-attack pushed the Germans back by 1–1.5km.

The intensity of the fighting grew on the second day. With the help of the Hetzers, the Germans occupied Jajgatópuszta (just north of Jákó) and Point 176 to the north-north-east. The 864th SPG Regiment arrived to meet them, directing the 2nd Battery north of Jákó towards Balaskópuzsta and the 1st, 3rd and 4th into Jákó. That day the regiment claimed to have knocked out a German assault gun and three towed guns.

German gains of the second day of the offensive were limited to just 2–4km on this part of the front. The lethargic pace of the offensive allowed the 57th Army to saturate the area around the German breakthough with thousands of anti-tank and anti-personnel mines, which greatly aided the defence. Nevertheless, the fighting was starting to take a toll on the 57th Army's armour. The 864th SPG Regiment lost one SU-76 destroyed, and one knocked out. One SU-76 was bogged down and left in no man's land. The knocked-out SU-76 was disabled by a friendly mine, which was not present on any Soviet maps or otherwise marked.

The nearby 1201st SPG Regiment (which had no SPGs but only T-34 tanks) lost seven of its T-34s burned and three knocked out on 7 March. According to the regiment's records, the cause of these losses was a powerful German artillery strike, which forced Soviet infantry to retreat and left them without cover. The T-34s conducted a fighting retreat through a muddy area where the Germans could not follow them, but took heavy losses in the process.

The 864th SPG Regiment continued to counter-attack alongside the 113th Rifle Division on 8 March. On that day the regiment claimed to have destroyed four enemy SPGs and one half-track at a cost of two SU-76s knocked out. Judging by the records of the regiment, it appears that they had only a vague idea of the enemy's strength. Enemy AFVs were continuously classified as 'tanks', even though the 2. Panzerarmee was armed only with assault guns at the time. It is no wonder that the report on the conclusion of the operation laments the insufficient work conducted by reconnaissance.

On 9 March the 1201st SPG Regiment turned its three remaining T-34s over to the 249th Tank Regiment and departed for Dombóvár where it would receive SU-76Ms instead. The 864th SPG Regiment continued to defend, having repaired one SPG for a total of 17 functional SU-76s and one T-34. The Germans attempted two attacks that day; both were beaten back. The 71. Infanterie-Division was only able to push slightly forward south of Jákó.

The 864th SPG Regiment kept fighting, leaving behind the 2nd Battery and moving to Csököly on 10 March where it deflected an enemy attack with the help of the 299th Rifle Division at the cost of one SU-76 burned out. The Soviet units were not the main focus of the German assault on that day, however, as elements of the 71. Infanterie-Division and the 16. SS-Panzergrenadier-Division were sent south to Kisbajom to probe the defences of the 1st Bulgarian Army there.

Help was also on its way to replace the recalled 1201st SPG Regiment. The 1891st SPG Regiment arrived in Baja with 21 SU-76s, and 21 more were brought in for the 1201st SPG Regiment, which was now located in Baté in reserve. These reserves were not meant to fight off the enemy attacks to the west, but rather to turn south and liquidate the Axis positions across the Drava.

The 864th SPG Regiment remained in its defensive positions on 11 March, deflecting another German attack at Csököly. The regiment spent most of the day repairing minor issues with its vehicles, refuelling, and restocking ammunition.

One T-34 and 18 SU-76s remained in the regiment's inventory: 16 in working order, one left in no man's land and one knocked out but recovered and undergoing medium repairs. At this point light SPGs made up the majority of Soviet armour fighting on the south-western axis, as the other armour elements of the 57th Army were kept in reserve (32nd Guards Mechanized Brigade, 1201st SPG Regiment,

OPPOSITE
This map shows the fighting at the southern end of Lake Balaton, 6–11 March 1945. Assault guns were a key component of the armoured forces on both sides. Despite fierce fighting, the Germans could not make a significant dent in Soviet defences. After regrouping and trying another attack northwards along the coast of Lake Balaton, the Germans gave up attacking in this direction on 17 March.

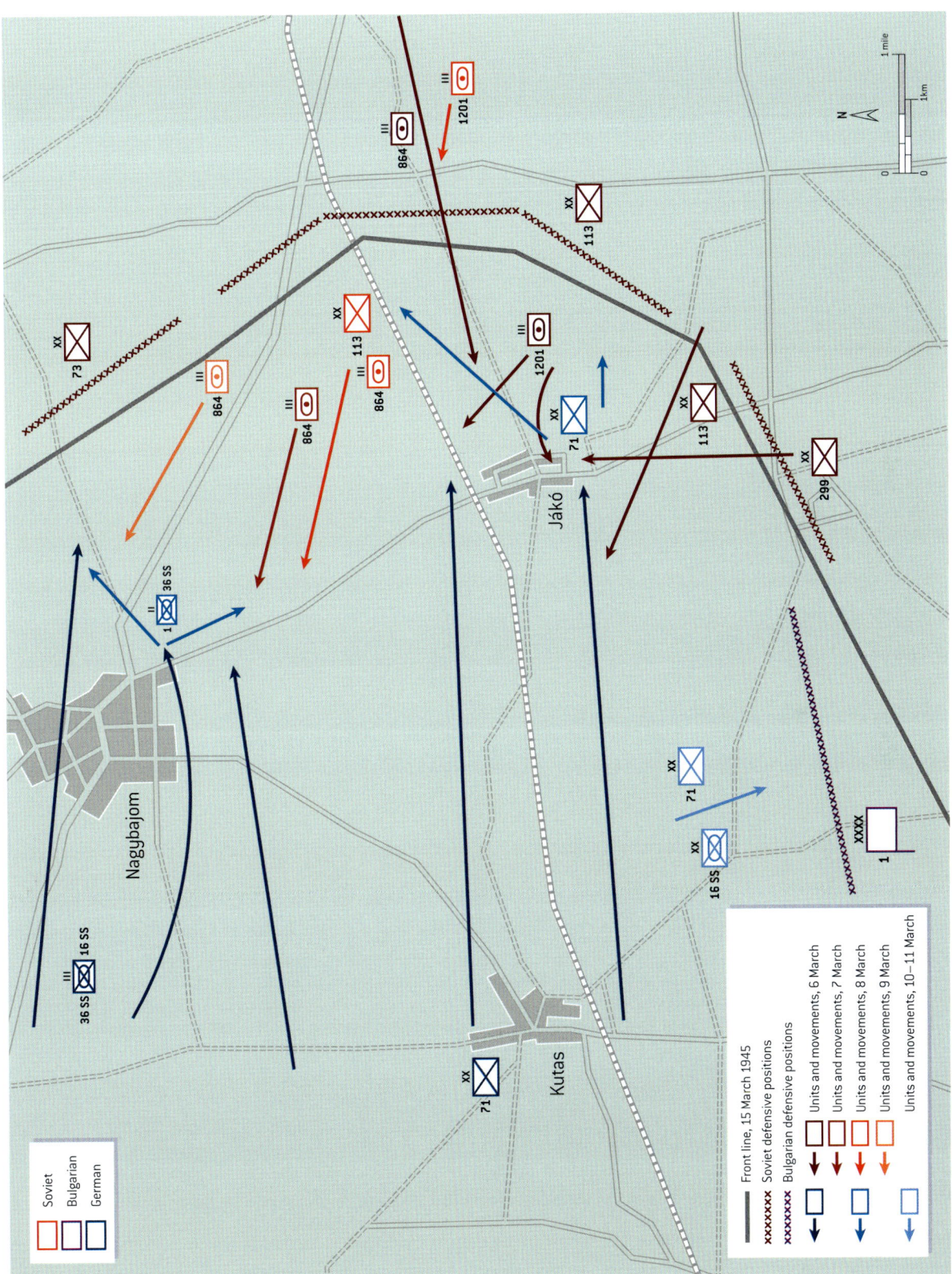

PREVIOUS PAGES

An SU-76M supporting Soviet infantry in urban combat. Soviet urban assault groups worked closely with artillery, and the SU-76M was more mobile and offered greater protection to its crew than a towed ZIS-3, making it perfect for this role. This was a symbiotic relationship. The lack of armour on the top and rear made the SU-76M vulnerable to attack by enemy infantry, meaning that the crew had to rely on the infantry it was supporting for protection to prevent the vehicle being hit from above or behind. Infantry also had to watch out for the blast of the SU-76M's gun, as the gases deflected by the muzzle brake could injure them at close range.

3rd Guards Motorcycle Regiment, 1891st SPG Regiment) or were in transit (53rd Guards Motorcycle Regiment). Only the 249th Tank Regiment (ten T-34s) was actively fighting. Thankfully, the 864th SPG Regiment was relieved by the 1201st SPG Regiment (one T-34, 20 SU-76s) on 13 March. Interestingly enough, the latter regiment could only put together two batteries worth of SU-76 crews; the rest of the SU-76s were operated by T-34 crewmen whose tanks had been lost in battle.

The 864th SPG Regiment was withdrawn into the reserves of the 64th Rifle Corps along with its 16 SU-76s. The vehicle abandoned in no man's land was not recovered and the vehicle undergoing medium repairs was not back in action. Three SU-76s were lost irretrievably during 6–12 March. In return, the 864th SPG Regiment claimed to have knocked out eight enemy tanks and SPGs.

The Germans also regrouped on 11–13 March. Attacking south and east proved fruitless, so orders were given to prepare for an attack to the north-east along the shore of Lake Balaton to link up with the I. Kavalleriekorps at Enying. An attack was attempted on 14 March against the 6th Guards Rifle Corps to the north at Nikla, but it proved to be no more effective than previous ones. The 864th SPG Regiment was once again ready to meet them, its SU-76s laying in ambush near Boronkai at 0800hrs on 15 March. The regiment lost the element of surprise, however, as two batteries were ordered to deploy to accompany a counter-attack by the 55th Rifle Regiment that was subsequently cancelled, but not before the Germans noticed the arrival of Soviet armour. A counter-attack was carried out at 1800hrs, during which one SU-76 was knocked out.

Further losses were suffered on the following day as the SU-76s were forced to relocate quickly to blunt enemy counter-attacks but without the ability to move undetected. One was lost on the march to artillery fire and two to air attack. In response, the SU-76s claimed to have destroyed three enemy AFVs, but another SU-76 was knocked out while repelling an enemy attack alongside the 55th Rifle Regiment. The SU-76s were then briefly withdrawn from the front line to perform harassing fire with migrating batteries, but on 16 March returned to their infantry-support role to defend against enemy attacks. Deployment of the 32nd Guards Mechanized Brigade and 20th Guards Rifle Division previously held in reserve made further attack in this direction unprofitable for the Germans. No further attempts were made to punch through Soviet defences here after 17 March.

A column of SU-76M assault guns in Hungary, 1945. A Lend-Lease jeep is also visible in the photo. (Keystone-France/Gamma-Keystone via Getty Images)

STATISTICS AND ANALYSIS

Soviet defences proved a tough nut to crack. Artillery, including SPGs such as the SU-76, was used in a very aggressive role. Rather than establishing a static gun belt, tanks were positioned in semi- or fully enclosed trenches that concealed Soviet guns from enemy observation and allowed them to strike at enemy flanks from close range. Reserve and false positions were also prepared, with single vehicles or guns used to make the false position appear more lifelike. When the enemy turned to fight this new-found threat, they would be hit in the flank by the real anti-tank defences. Anti-tank combat was a very important duty even for the SU-76, the crews of which were instructed to ignore all other targets in favour of enemy tanks when those appeared, resuming their prior mission only when the tanks had been destroyed or suppressed. A wide variety of illumination tools including flares, incendiary shells and spotlights allowed the Red Army to fight effectively even at night.

The Hetzer also had to fight in roles for which it was not originally intended. Rather than serving as tank destroyers, most Hetzers at Lake Balaton performed the role of assault guns, supporting infantry attacks. In this role the Hetzer's thick frontal armour and high-velocity anti-tank gun offered few benefits, while reduced situational awareness resulting from poor visibility and poor off-road mobility due to its narrow tracks and insufficiently powerful engine for its weight were very detrimental. German troops often listed mud as an excuse for why Hetzers could not be in a position where they were most needed. Being forced to move on roads also meant that Hetzers suffered major damage from mines. In cases where Hetzers did arrive on the battlefield, they were used effectively to help infantry forces advance.

An SU-76M in Berlin, 1945. A spare wheel and track link hang on the upper front hull where they could serve as improvised armour if hit. (Imwar/Alamy Stock Photo)

Engagements like these show how important it is to treat an AFV as a cog in a war machine rather than a single unit. While in the northern sector between lakes Balaton and Velence a mix of armour was used, the south-western sector was much more homogeneous when it came to AFVs, with the Soviet side fighting mostly in SU-76Ms and the Germans in StuGs and Hetzers. This allows us to examine their performance in relative isolation.

The 57th Army mainly employed SU-76Ms during the fighting at the south-western end of Lake Balaton during most of the battle, while the Germans used StuGs and Hetzers with their thicker armour and more powerful guns. In a direct confrontation, one would no doubt choose the Hetzer as the likely winner, and yet the Germans made hardly any progress against Soviet defences after the SU-76M entered the battle. The Red Army was effectively able to play to the strengths of the SU-76M, deploying it in areas where artillery support was needed most to reinforce its infantry. While the SU-76M could face StuGs and Hetzers in a head-on confrontation with manageable losses, this was generally avoided as the firepower of the mobile assault guns could be better used when accompanying infantry counter-attacks. It is interesting to note that while the Germans constantly complained about their ability to deploy assault guns being limited by mud, Soviet SU-76 units judged the roads to be suitable for travel by all types of vehicles and did not appear to be impeded by the terrain. This was also true in other areas of the 3rd Ukrainian Front, as the 208th SPG Brigade described their sector as generally favourable for the use of tank forces.

According to Soviet reports, the Germans perceived Soviet SPGs as a serious threat. Revealing the positions of SU-76s was liable to attract a severe bombardment, as a result of which it was wise to change positions immediately after firing. This was not a big problem when supporting counter-attacks (which were frequent even though the Red Army was nominally defending) but during defensive fighting required the preparation of multiple back-up positions. It was noted that when digging trenches to

Hetzer displayed next to a mannequin at the Oorlogsmuseum Overloon. This photograph allows one to appreciate the low height of the vehicle – only slightly taller than an adult male – which made it very easy to hide in an ambush. This came at the cost of a very low fighting compartment, however, in which the crew could not stand up. When used in an offensive role, the Hetzer's low profile presented fewer advantages, but its disadvantages remained just as severe. (Author)

hide SPGs from observation and artillery, the trenches should be large enough to allow the vehicle to turn 360 degrees in order to fire on any nearby targets. It was also considered reasonable to link SPG positions with infantry trenches via passageways, if time permitted. As often happened with SPGs, however, infantry commanders attempted to use them as ersatz tanks. SPG commanders noted that it would be useful to have a bow machine gun to combat enemy infantry.

The 3rd Ukrainian Front weathered the German attack well. Between 6 and 16 March, only one shipment of reinforcements arrived: 75 SU-76s, 20 Shermans and 20 T-34s. While other units were attached to the Front by 16 March, they did not take part in the defensive fighting and were only there to participate in the counter-offensive. The rest of the Front's losses could be compensated for in part by repairing damaged vehicles. Total losses on the Soviet side consisted of 165 tanks and SPGs. The Germans claimed 203 Soviet tracked AFVs destroyed and captured during this time, which is fairly close. Of those, the majority were T-34s, 84 of which were lost. SU-76 losses included 11 in the 18th Tank Corps, three in the 5th Cavalry Corps and 11 in the 864th SPG Regiment, for a total of 25 SPGs. The 1896th SPG Regiment of the 5th Cavalry Corps also reported two SU-76 that needed medium repairs; one SPG in the 864th SPG Regiment was undergoing light repairs. Even though the majority of SU-76 units (with the exception of those attached to the 4th Guards Army) fought at the front lines in areas where German breakthroughs were deepest and fighting was particularly fierce, this accounts for only one-quarter of the original number of SPGs available as total losses, while 60 per cent of the arguably better-armoured and -armed T-34s and T-34-85s were lost.

German losses were more severe. While the Germans reported the total loss of just 42 tanks and SPGs and one armoured personnel carrier (other sources give an even lower number: 31 tanks and SPGs), these figures are remarkably low for such a disastrous operational failure. The true scale of the damage done can be appreciated from readiness figures. For example, while the 2. SS-Panzer-Division reported only five total losses among its Jagdpanzers during 6–13 March, only 17 out 56 vehicles not written off were reported as being combat ready. Similarly, the III. Panzerkorps reported just seven tanks written off (one PzKpfw IV and six Panthers) but the total

SU-76Ms moving into Germany, winter 1945. Operation *Spring Awakening* achieved very little in terms of delaying the Red Army in its advance towards the German capital and the country's industrial regions. (Pictorial Press Ltd/Alamy Stock Photo)

number of combat-ready tanks, assault guns and Jagdpanzers declined from 153 to 63 in the same time period.

After the battle, a Soviet trophy commission marked each German vehicle individually with a sequential number. The commission reported examining 968 knocked-out and abandoned AFVs on the battlefield and photographing 400 that were of particular interest. A total of 279 photographs of destroyed German tanks at Lake Balaton are known today, with '355' as the highest visible painted inventory number. The Soviet estimate of 324 German tanks and SPGs and 120 armoured personnel carriers destroyed or knocked out or captured during the Lake Balaton operation by elements of the 3rd Ukrainian Front could be inflated, but judging by the photographic evidence it appears to be much closer to the truth than the German figures.

The destruction of a considerable part of Heeresgruppe Süd's armour had the opposite effect that Operation *Spring Awakening* had intended. Rather than protecting one of Germany's few remaining allies and shoring up the defences of Austria, Czechia and southern Germany, this defeat meant that the Germans were no longer able to protect themselves effectively on this axis. Limited use of reserves in the defensive fighting at Lake Balaton meant that the 3rd Ukrainian Front was immediately able to launch a counter-offensive: the Vienna Offensive Operation. In just a month, the Front swept through Hungary and into Austria, taking Vienna. The offensive was originally planned for 15 March, meaning that the incredible amount of forces the Germans had built up had a negligible effect on Soviet operational planning, delaying the offensive only by a couple of days.

AFTERMATH

The SU-76M was a promising chassis, it being possible to modernize it with more powerful weapons Indeed, the idea of equipping the SU-76 with a 57mm ZIS-2 gun had been voiced in response to the appearance of the Tiger heavy tank. This conversion would have been easy to accomplish, as the ZIS-2 and 76mm ZIS-3 guns shared a carriage. The vehicle (designated the SU-57) was built, tested and put forward for production in 1944. A decree putting the SU-57 into production starting in September 1944 was composed, but never signed. The Red Army had lost interest in the ZIS-2 gun as a prospective weapon back in the autumn of 1943, when it was established that it could not penetrate the frontal armour of the Panther tank or Ferdinand tank destroyer.

This was only the beginning, however, and work on a SU-76M equipped with an even more powerful 85mm gun began in the spring of 1944. The D-5S-85 gun installed in the SU-85 could be adapted for a much lighter chassis. Like the SU-57, this vehicle (called SU-85A) was built in the summer of 1944. While the gun had issues, the prototype proved that the SU-76M chassis could be loaded to 12 tonnes in the process of modernization. The improved SU-85B was built in the spring of 1945 with a more compact 85mm V-13 gun. GAZ was beginning to wind down work on military projects, however, and focus on civilian manufacturing. Even though the SU-85B passed trials in the autumn of 1945, it never entered production. As a result, no new light SPG went into production when the last SU-76M left the assembly line in October 1945. The SU-76M remained in service with the Red Army (Soviet Army from 25 February 1946) as well as in the armies of Poland, Romania, Czechoslovakia, Afghanistan, North Korea, China and North Vietnam. While the SU-76M in Europe finished its career peacefully, the examples in service in Asia saw active use in the Korean War (1950–53) and beyond.

The SU-76M continued to serve in many nations aligned with the Soviet Union after the end of World War II. This example was captured by US forces during the Korean War. (US Signal Corps Archive)

In comparison, the Jagdpanzer 38 did not enjoy much post-war success. Even though Škoda had 1,200 partially completed vehicles on hand at the end of the war, the firm had trouble finding customers. The vehicles were first offered to the Soviet Union, which refused to accept them. The tank destroyer piqued the interest of the Swiss, who were already using Czechoslovakian Praga LTL-H tanks under the designation Pzkw 39. Eight Jagdpanzer 38s were sold to Switzerland in August 1946, where they were used under the factory designation G-13. An order for 100 more followed in November. Owing to a shortage of 7.5cm PaK 39 guns, these vehicles were equipped with 7.5cm PaK 40 guns, which could be installed with some modifications to the vehicle. Starting with the 65th vehicle, the Swiss G-13s were fitted with new 148PS Sauer Arbon diesel engines instead of the Praga AE. Another order for 50 G-13s was placed in 1947. The 158 G-13s served in the Swiss Army until 1968.

An SU-76M in Budapest, 1956. Even though improved light SPGs were developed, the SU-76M remained in service with the Soviet Army and the armies of Soviet-aligned countries. (Fortepan 24695/Wikimedia/ CC BY-SA 3.0)

A Hetzer abandoned by the roadside. Oil leaking out of the maintenance hatch and an open toolbox on the engine deck suggests that this vehicle may have been abandoned due to mechanical failure rather than battle damage. (Imwar/Alamy Stock Photo)

Czechoslovakia kept the Jagdpanzer 38 in service after the war under the designation ST-I. Over 300 vehicles of this type were marshalled in 1945–46. They were either brand new or used, but the latter were in good enough condition to be returned to service. ČKD was tasked with the completion and refurbishment of 50 ST-Is in 1946. In 1947, 20 more ST-Is were ordered from Škoda, and a further 30 in 1949. A training vehicle, designated ST-III, was also built on the chassis of the Jagdpanzer 38. The gun was removed and replaced with a seat for an instructor; a superstructure was added to the top of the hull; and a large portion of the armour plate in front of the driver was cut out and replaced with a new observation device. An order for 50 ST-IIIs was placed with ČKD. As a result, Czechoslovakia had 246 ST-Is and ST-IIIs as well as three Bergepanzer 38 ARVs in service by the start of 1949, with 150 of these being newly built or freshly refurbished. They did not last long, however, and were phased out of service in the early 1950s. A flamethrower tank, the PM-1, was built on the chassis of the ST-I and tested in the early 1950s, but the Czechoslovak Army lost interest in the project. Neither the Swiss nor Czechoslovakian vehicles were used in combat and are therefore now fairly common in museums and in the hands of private collectors.

GLOSSARY

AFV Armoured fighting vehicle.
APCR Armour Piercing, Composite, Rigid. An armour-penetrating projectile consisting of a tungsten-carbide core inside a lightweight sabot.
ARV Armoured Recovery Vehicle
ČKD *Českomoravská-Kolben-Daněk*. An engineering company in Prague that designed and built the LT vz.38 tank and other vehicles on its chassis. The company was known as **BMM** (Böhmisch-Mährische Maschinenfabrik AG) under German occupation.
GABTU *Glavnoye Avtobronetankovoye Upravleniye* (Main Automobile and Armour Directorate).
GAU *Glavnoye Artilleriyskoye Upravleniye* (Main Artillery Directorate). This directorate of the Red Army was responsible for the development of towed and self-propelled artillery.
GAVTU *Glavnoye Avtomobilnyoe Upravleniye* (Main Automobile Directorate).
GAZ *Gorkovsky Avto-Zavod* (Gorky Automobile Factory). Producer and developer of light tanks and subsequently light SPGs.
GBTU *Glavnoye Brone Tankovoe Upravleniye* (Main Armour Directorate).
GKO *Gosudarstvenniy Komitet Oborony* (State Committee of Defence). The Soviet government organization in charge of all issues relating to war.
HE High explosive
Hetzer The Jagdpanzer 38 tank destroyer's unofficial nickname. The term is often translated as 'hunter' but refers specifically to persistence hunting.
Jagdpanzer Literally 'tank hunter', an armoured vehicle developed primarily as a tank destroyer.
MIAG *Mühlenbau und Industrie Aktiengesellschaft* (mechanical engineering company based in Braunschweig).
NKTP *Narodniy Kommissariat Tankovoy Promyshlennosti* (People's Commissariat of Tank Production). The Soviet ministry responsible for the production of all tracked armoured vehicles.
OKH *Oberkommando des Heeres* (Army High Command).
PaK *Panzerabwehrkanone* (anti-tank gun). The designation used both for towed guns and guns installed in German SPGs.
Panzerwaffe Armoured branch, German armed forces.
SPAAG Self-propelled anti-aircraft gun.
SPG Self-propelled gun.
SU *Samokhodnaya Ustanovka* (self-propelled gun mount). The term used as a part of the designation of all Soviet SPGs.
UMM *Upravleniye Motorizatzii i Mekhanizatzii* (Directorate of Mechanization and Motorization).
USA (Self-Propelled Artillery Directorate).
UZTM *Uralskiy Zavod Tyazhelogo Mashinostroyeniya* (Ural Heavy Machinebuilding Factory).
VOMAG *Vogtländische Maschinenfabrik Aktiengesellschaft* (automobile manufacturing company based in Plauen).
ZIS *Zavod imeni Stalina* (Stalin factory in Moscow). Producer of, among others, the ZIS-3 gun used in the SU-76 and SU-76M.

BIBLIOGRAPHY

Baryatinksiy, M. (2009). *Slavyanskaya bronya Gitlera*. Moscow: Eksmo.
Canadian Military Headquarters, London (CMHQ), Files Block No. 55 - 5777, Images 2481-2490, Preliminary Notes on Pz.Jag. für 7.5 cm PaK 39 (L.48).
Canadian Military Headquarters, London (CMHQ), Files Block No. 55 - 5788, Image 3423.

Chubachin, A. (2009). *SU-76 Bratskaya mogila ekipazha ili oruzhiye Pobedy?*. Moscow: Eksmo.

Combat journal of the Armoured and Mechanized Forces of the 3rd Ukrainian Front, TsAMO RF F.243 Op.2928 D.131 L.1.

Compendium of reports 'Defensive operation of the 3rd Ukrainian Front in January-March 1945', TsAMO RF F.243 D.2900 L.1.

Drig, Ye. (2020). *Stalinskiye Tankisty*. Moscow: Russikiye Vityazi.

Falk, Victor A. (2016). *Of Fire, Iron and Blood A Short History of the Royal Hungarian "Honved" Army in the Second World War*. Cleveland, OH: Self-Published.

Isayev, A.V. & Kolomiets, M.V. (2009). *Razgrom 6-y tankovoy armii SS*. Moscow: Yauza.

Kerekes, András (2015). *The Role and Creation of the Royal Hungarian Assault Artillery, and the Zrínyi II Assault Howitzer*. Hadmérnök. 10 (2), 75-88, 2015. ISSN: 1788-1919.

Mujzer, Dr Peter (2000). *The Royal Hungarian Army, 1920–1945 Volume II: Hungarian Mobile Forces*. Bayside, NY: Axis Europa Books.

Office of the Chief Ordnance Officer, ETO Ordnance Technical Intelligence Report No.183 Translation of German Manual on 7.5cm Assault Gun (le. Pz. Jag. 38).

'Orders to commanders of the 4th Ukrainian Front on the combat use of SPG regiments (SU-76) and their cooperation with infantry in combat'. Collection of Combat Documents from the Great Patriotic War, vol. 2, doc. 10.

Pasholok, Y. *Bestseller iz Pragi*. Available at https://warspot.ru/8148-bestseller-iz-pragi (accessed 28 October 2024).

Pasholok, Y. *Finalnaya versiya*. Available at https://warspot.ru/13258-finalnaya-versiya (accessed 28 October 2024).

Pasholok, Y. *Glavniy Konstruktor 30-kh*. Available at https://warspot.ru/16472-glavnyy-konstruktor-30-h (accessed 28 October 2024).

Pasholok, Y. *Mytishinekaya krysha dlya SU-76M*. Available at https://dzen.ru/a/X3wDV5UsOzcO12KQ?sid=214708974018530560 (accessed 28 October 2024).

Pasholok, Y. *Na puti k SU-76*. Available at https://warspot.ru/8037-na-puti-k-su-76 (accessed 28 October 2024).

Pasholok, Y. *Nemetskiy istrebitel na chehoslovatskoy baze*. Available at https://warspot.ru/9759-nemetckiy-istrebitel-na-chehoslovatckoy-baze (accessed 28 October 2024).

Pasholok, Y. *Nenuzniy razvedchik*. Available at https://warspot.ru/4357-nenuzhnyy-razvedchik (accessed 28 October 2024).

Pasholok, Y. *Rokovaya samokhodka*. Available at https://warspot.ru/10270-rokovaya-samohodka (accessed 28 October 2024).

Pasholok, Y. *Samiy massoviy samokhod Krasnoy armii*. Available at https://warspot.ru/11958-samyy-massovyy-samohod-krasnoy-armii (accessed 28 October 2024).

Pasholok, Y. *V polushage ot SU-76M*. Available at https://dzen.ru/a/ZH8J7K35Yz0bp31p?sid=73621548879939 (accessed 28 October 2024).

Pejčoch, Ivo (2009). Československá těžká vojenská technika, Vývoj, výroba, nasazení a export československých tanků, obrněných automobilů a pásových dělostřeleckých tahačů 1918-1956. Institute of Czech History.

Raths, R. *Hetzer's gonna hetz - but what EXACTLY is hetz?* Available at https://www.youtube.com/watch?v=SJGkovFT2VM (accessed 28 October 2024).

Reichsministers f. Rüstung u. Kriegsproduktion. *Dokumentation W 127: Datenblätter für Heeres-Waffen, Fahrzeuge, Gerät*.

Report on the condition of the Armoured and Mechanized Forces materiel of the 3rd Ukrainian Front. TsAMO RF F.243 Op.2900 D.2001 L.52.

Reynolds, M. (2013). *Sons of the Reich II SS Panzer Corps*. Barnsley: Pen and Sword.

Svirin, M., Baronov, O., Kolomiyets, M. & Nedogonov, D. (1999). *Boï u ozera Balaton*. Moscow: Exprint.

Szamveber, N. (2020). *Last Panzer Battles in Hungary*. Keszthely: PeKo Publishing.

Tank Front, *Organizatsiya samokhodno-artilleriyskikh chastey*. Available at http://tankfront.ru/ussr/organisation/org_sa.html (accessed 28 October 2024).

Zaitsev, D. *Posledniye tanki Tretyego reiha*. Available at https://warspot.ru/5081-poslednie-tanki-tretiego-reyha (accessed 28 October 2024).

INDEX

References to illustrations are shown in **bold**.

AH-IV/-IV-Sv light tank/tankette 18
Armeekorps: LXVIII. 51; XCI. 55
armies (Sov): 1st Guards 28; 4th Guards 24, 25, 26, 28, 48, 55, 62, 73; 26th **27**, 28, 48, 55, 58, 59, 64; 27th **27**, 28, 48, 59, 64; 57th **27**, 28, 48, 55, 62, 65, 66, 70, 72
artillery forces: (Ger) 28, 55, 65, 66, 70; (Sov) 10, 25, 29, 46, 55, 58, 63, 65
artillery/agricultural tractors 9
AT-1 artillery tank 10
Aufklärer 38D reconnaissance tank 21
Austria, Soviet threat to 24, 64, 74

Bergepanzer 38 ARV 21, 22, 50, 77
Bulgarian Army 4–5, 24, 26, 28, 55, 66, **67**

cavalry forces (Ger): I. Kavalleriekorps 26, **27**, 55, 58, 62, 64, 70; 3./4. Kavallerie-Dvn 62, 63
cavalry forces (Sov): bns 62; corps 47: 5th Guards 28, 48, 62; dvns: 11th/12th/63rd 62; regts: 41st/43rd 62
Czechoslovakia, fighting in 16, 24, 26, **45**
Czechoslovakian Army 16, 18, 19

Ferdinand tank destroyer 75
Flammpanzer 38 flamethrower tank 22

G-13 tank destroyer **7**, 22, **32**, **33**, 76
GAZ-71 SPG 12
Germany, fighting in 31, **47**, **52**, 64, 74
Ginzburg, Semyon A. 9, 10–11, 12, 13
Grille SPG 5
Grosstraktor 10

Heeresgruppen (Ger): E 26; Mitte 4, 25; Süd 28, 58, 59, 74
Hungarian Army 7, 26, **27**, 55, 62, 64
  20th Assault Artillery Battalion **23**, 63, 64
Hungary (Operation *Spring Awakening*) 4–5, 7, **15**, **23**, 24–26, **27**, 28–29, **48**, 51, **53**, 55, **56–57**, 58–59, 62–66, **67**, **68–69**, 70, **70**, 74

Jagdpanther tank destroyer 26
Jagdpanzer IV tank destroyer 19, 42
Jagdpanzer 38 Hetzer tank destroyer 17, 72, 77
  armament 5, 20, **22**, **35**, 36, 38, **38**, 40–41, 42, 61, 71, 72: ammunition **35**, 36, **37**, **38**, 41, 61
  features 22, **23**, 32, **38**, 40–41, **40**, **41**, 45, **63**: armour protection 5, 20, **21**, **22**, 32, **32**, **33**, 38, 51, 58, 60, 71, 72; crew/crew stations 40–42, **40**, **41**, 50, 51, **56–57**, 60, 62, 73; crew training 50, 51; design shortcomings 25, 40, **40**, **41**, 58, 60, 71, 73; engine 44–45, 58, 71; gunsight 32, 40, **51**, **61**; running gear 44, **44**, **45**, 58, **63**; vision devices 40, **40**, 42, 50, **51**, 59, 60
  importance/effectiveness of 6, 38
  origins/development 5, 16–17
  production 7, 20–21, 22
  use/users 7, 20–21, 22, **23**, **25**, 37, 50–51, **61**, 62, 63, 64, 65, 72, **73**: as assault guns 6, **56–57**, 71; for infantry support **56–57**, 60, 62, 63, 64, 73, 74, 77; losses 45, 62, 63, 64, 73, 74, **77**; post-war users 7, 22, **32**, **33**, 76–77
Jagdpanzer 38 Starr tank destroyer 20, 22
Jagdpanzer 38D tank destroyer 21–22

KH-60 light tank 18
Korean War **45**, 75, **76**
Kugelblitz 38D SPAAG 21
KV-1/-1S heavy tanks 10, 17, 58

leichter Panzerjäger auf 38(t) 7, 17
Lithuania, light tanks for 18
LT vz.34/vz.35 light tanks 16, 18, 19
LT vz.38 light tank 5, 16, 17, 19
LTL/LTP light tanks 18
LTL-H tank destroyer 18, 76
Luchs reconnaissance tank 16

M4A2 Sherman medium tank 28, 73
Marder III tank destroyer 5, 51

North Korean Army, SPGs for **45**, **76**

P-I tankette 18
P-II light tank 18
PaK 40 auf Pz.Kpw.38(t) 17
PaK 43/3 auf Sfl.38 (Ausf.M) Motor vorn 17
Panther medium tank 20, 73, 75
Panzer forces (Ger): armies: 2. 51, 55, 64, 65, 66; 6. SS 26, 28, 55, 64; corps: I. SS 26, **27**, 55, 62, 64; II. SS 26, 55, 63; III. 55, 63, 73–74; IV. SS 25; dvns: 1. *Leibstandarte Adolf Hitler* 26, 55; 2. SS **27**, 73; 3. 26, **27**; 3. SS *Totenkopf* 26; 23. 26; 12. *Hitlerjugend* 55
Panzerjäger 38(t) tank destroyer 19
Panzerjäger-Abteilungen: 171./175./188./255 50–51; 501./509./560 29; 731. 50; *Feldherrnhalle* 26
Panzerwagen 39 tank destroyer 18, 76
Peruvian Army, light tanks for 18
PM-1 flamethrower tank 7
PzKpfw II light tank 16
PzKpfw III/IV medium tanks 16, 17, 73
PzKpfw 38(t) light tank 5, 7, 16, 17, **17**, 18, 10
PzKpfw 38(t)-18 main destroyer 17, 19–20
PzKpfw 38(t) nA reconnaissance tank 7, 16, 19, 32, 44
PzSfl 2 tank destroyer 17

S-II-a light tank 18
Schukin, M.N. 11, 12, 13
SP artillery brigades (Sov): 208th 28
SP artillery regiments (Sov): 366th 28
SP-126 light tank 10
SPG forces (Sov): bdes 47: 208th 48, 63, 59, 72; bns 47: 8th/13th/44th Guards 48; 72nd **27**, 48, 58; 75th/88th/122nd 48; 432nd **27**, 48, 59; btys 46, 47, 58, 59, 62, 65, 66, 70; regts 4–6, 47: 864th **27**, 48, 65, 66, **67**, 70, 73: 1016th 48, 59, 63; 1201st 66, **67**, 70; 1202nd **27**, 48, 58, 59; 1438th 48, 58–59; 1891st 48, 62, 66, 70; 1896th **27**, 48, 62, 73
ST-I/-III tank destroyers 77
Strv m/37 and m/41 light tanks 18
Sturmgeschütz assault guns (Ger) 20, 26, 28, 62, 65, 66, 72, 74
Sturmgeschütz-Brigaden: 261. 28; 303. 26
Sturmhaubitzen (Ger) 21, 26, 28
SU-5/-6 SPGs 10
SU-11 SPAAG 7, 11, 12, **12**
SU-12 SPG 7, **9**, 11–12, 13
SU-14 SPG 10
SU-15/-15M SPGs 7, 13, **13**, 14

SU-16 SPG 14
SU-31 SPAAG 7, 11, 12
SU-32 SPG 7, 11
SU-38 SPG 13, 14
SU-57 SPG 75
SU-74 SPG 13, 14
SU-76/-76M SPGs 11, 13, 43, 44, 58, 61
  armament 5, 12, 16, 28, 30, 31, **31**, 32, 33, **34**, 36, **36**, 37, 38, **39**, 40, 42, 60, 65, 70, 75: ammunition 33, **34**, **36**, **37**, 38, 45, 60, **65**
  features **9**, 13, **13**, 14, **14**, **15**, 16, 30, **31**, 39, **39**, **43**, **49**, 75: armour protection 14, 16, 30, 31, 32, 38, 61, 70; crew/crew stations 5, 30, 39–40, **39**, 42, 59, **68–69**, 70, 71; crew training 10, 48–49, 59; design shortcomings 12, 14, 31, 70; engine 43; gunsight 14, **60**; improvements/modernization 14, 16; running gear 43, **43**; vision devices 39, **39**, 42, **49**
  origins/development 5, 7, 11–12, 13, 14
  production 11–12, 13, 14, 16, 43, 46–47
  use/users 5–6, **15**, 16, **27**, 28, 37, 46, 47–48, 58, **60**, **61**, 62, 63, 65, 66, **70**, 71, 72–73, **74**, **76**: as ersatz tanks 59, 73; for infantry support/urban combat **5**, **29**, **31**, **47**, **52**, **68–69**, 70, 72; kills **31**, 58, 59, 61, 66, 70, 73; losses 31, 58, 59, 61, 66, 70, 73; post-war users **45**, 75, **76**, **76**
SU-85A/-85B SPGs 58, 75
SU-100 tank destroyer 28, 59
SU-122 SPG 46
Surin, Aleksey M. 5, 16, 17, 18–19, 45
Sweden, tank destroyers for 18, 19
Switzerland, tank destroyers for 18, 76

T-18 (MS-1)/T-19/T-20 light tanks 10
T-26 light tank and T-26-4 artillery tank 10
T-28 medium tank 10
T-30 heavy tank 8
T-34/-34-85 medium tanks 6, 8, 10, 11, 17, 19, 28, 58, 66, 70, 73
T-35 heavy tank 10
T-37 light tank 10
T-40 amphibious reconnaissance tank 8
T-46 light tank 10
T-50 light tank 8, 10, 11
T-60 light tank 7, 8–9, 10, 11
T-70 light tank 5, 7, 9, **9**, 11, 28, 47
T-70B 11, 13, 30, 43
Tančík vz.33 tankette 18
tank forces (Sov): armies/bns 47, 59; bdes: 32nd 11; 170th 58; corps 47: 18th **27**, 28, 48, 58–59, 63, 73; 23rd 28; dvns 25; regts: 22nd 58; 249th 66, 70
Tanque 39 light tank 18
Tiger heavy tank 6, 20, 26, 59, 75
TNH/TNH-S/TNH-Sv light tanks 18, 19

Ukrainian fronts: 2nd 24, 26; 3rd 4–5, 24, 25, 26, 28, 47–48, 49, 58, 62, 63, 72, 73, 74; 4th 24

Vickers: light/medium tanks 10; tankettes 18

Wöhler, General der Infanterie Otto 58, 64

Yugoslavian Army 5, 24, 26

ZSU-37 SPAAG 12